Access Services : A Handbook

To my parents and Jean

Access Services
A Handbook

by

Ann Catherine Paietta

McFarland & Company, Inc., Publishers
Jefferson, North Carolina

Library Association Publishing
London, England

British Library Cataloguing in Publication Data

Paietta, Ann Catherine
  Access services : a handbook.
  I. Title
  025

    ISBN 1-85604-034-8

Library of Congress Cataloguing-in-Publication Data

Paietta, Ann Catherine, 1956–
    Access services : a handbook / Ann Catherine Paietta.
      p.   cm.
    Includes bibliographical references and index.
    ISBN 0-89950-599-6 (lib. bdg. : 50# alk. paper) ∞
    1. Libraries and readers—Handbooks, manuals, etc.   2. Libraries—
Circulation, loans—Handbooks, manuals, etc.   3. Library materials—
Access control—Handbooks, manuals, etc.   4. Libraries—Security
measures—Handbooks, manuals, etc.   5. Open and closed shelves—
Handbooks, manuals, etc.   I. Title.
Z711.P26   1991
025.6—dc20   90-53601
                                                                          CIP

Manufactured in the United States of America

McFarland & Company, Inc., Publishers
Box 611, Jefferson, North Carolina 28640

Published in the United Kingdom by
Library Association Publishing Ltd.,
7 Ridgmount Street, London WC1E 7AE

Acknowledgments

During the writing of this book, the Yale University Harvey Cushing/John Hay Whitney Medical Library underwent a two and one-half year renovation project. I learned more from these trying but rewarding times than I ever thought possible.

My library experience is primarily with academic libraries but this book is applicable to any library.

I want to thank Judy Parker of Seeley Mudd Library, Yale University, for her assistance with Chapter 4, Stack Management. She helped me get the book off the ground.

I spent so many hours writing this book because of my conviction that access services are critical to the proper operation of libraries.

Also, I want to thank the staff at the Medical Library for their support. Thanks to Jean Kauppila and Terry Johnson for providing editing assistance. And a warm thanks to Bella Berson, the retired associate university librarian and director of the Medical Library.

Table of Contents

Table of Figures

Table of Figures

Introduction

What Are Access Services?

Access services comprise those functions that facilitate patrons' access to a library's collection in all its formats—nonprint, sound, video, print, electronic, or graphics. Notably, access services include traditional duties such as circulating and shelving materials, maintaining photocopiers, and processing interlibrary loan requests. The description cannot be applied without exception but the duties mentioned should be performed by some department of the library and in many libraries they are assigned to access services.

Access services affect almost every aspect of the library, from preventing theft or mutilation of materials to contributing statistics for collection development. The staff deal with social issues such as latchkey children, the homeless, censorship, or privileged information. There are always access services staff present when the library is open. For example, in the event of inclement weather, a skeleton crew may run the library and usually that crew consists of access services staff. Traditionally the role of the library has been to furnish access to print materials, but now, electronic systems, computer databases and nonprint materials come into play. Today, few patrons can afford everything they need for research, entertainment, or education. Even in the future, access to information by means of libraries must continue to be made available. For example, on-line journal article retrieval may become economically feasible for individuals, but in many situations the print version will still need to be perused. Also, there will always be segments of the population who will be either unable or unwilling to purchase the technology.

Along with a mandatory photocopying operation, stack management, and circulation desk operation, other responsibilities come under the charge of access services. With the escalating cost of materials, access services have become valuable as a means to assist collection development decision making. Libraries across the country are establishing telefacsimile links to each other.

Access services play the central role in the dissemination of information while bridging technical and reference services. The information services offered by the library are what distinguish it from a warehouse. You must remind yourself that patrons are those whom the library serves. To achieve a high level of service, you must constantly view all library services through patrons' eyes. For example, the library must be useful to children as well as adults.

The Chapters

This book examines how access services link public and technical services while maintaining their own identity. Typically, you will find technical services unappreciative of the front line and reference not fully understanding the behind-the-scenes activities. The individual working in access services faces the dual role of serving a diverse audience as well as working with the behind-the-scenes staff. Access services people perform those duties that when correctly done few ever think about. The role of the access services department is also to augment the information used for collection development policies regarding both selection and weeding. The collection development for your library depends on your library's mission statement. Will you keep only current journals or a comprehensive collection? Statistics, developed by access services staff, that are based on patron use as opposed to guessing can better assist in determining the number of copies of a particular item to purchase. The access services staff provide reference service at the circulation desk and in the stacks. To be the person in charge of the unit demands knowledge of librarianship, communication skills, and management techniques.

Chapter 1 deals with one of the fundamental functions of access services, control over the circulation of materials. The circulation, or loan, desk has come to symbolize this particular component. This chapter emphasizes technology and the demand it creates on circulation. No matter what occurs down the road, circulation control of library materials must be sustained.

Computer databases, end-user computing, telefacsimile transmission, and other electronic advances open up resources to patrons. This creates easier access to information sources and thereby increases the need for delivery services. Chapter 2 discusses the traditional methods of interlibrary loan and photocopying operations as well as the impact of technology, such as telefacsimile transmission, on information delivery. Undeniably, there are changes abroad that greatly influence information delivery services. There is no way that one library can keep up with the output of publishers and universities. In this time of "I want it yesterday" and escalating costs, information delivery has become an even more integral service.

Chapter 3 focuses on the disquieting responsibilities of patrons, security, and the confidentiality of information and library records. Recently, the library world has been filled with information about the 80s and 90s FBI investigation of libraries and spies—the "Library Awareness Program." This federal agency was attempting to determine what materials spies or subversives or suspicious persons used and if librarians were influenced into cooperating with such individuals. Librarians who refused to divulge library use records had their backgrounds checked to determine whether they were themselves collaborators. With libraries in many locations, and open evenings and weekends, all levels of staff need nowadays to be especially prepared for the handling of any number of troubling encounters with patrons or overzealous government agents. Libraries are not immune to society's ailments. Chapter 3 also addresses a number of social issues, such as latchkey children and the homeless, which impact libraries.

No matter how many citations are in hand, if patrons cannot locate the material it becomes a wish list. The condition of the stacks and the helpfulness of the staff are usually what patrons remember after they leave the library. Access services staff must be conscious of this public service role. The attitude of "just a shelver" needs to be replaced with "backbone of the library." Chapter 4 addresses the critical function of stack management, and includes topics such as the electronic spreadsheet, arrangement of materials, preservation, equipment choices, training, and planning.

The most important resource of the library is its staff—the people who supply the library with their work, creativity, and drive. Without an educated, trained, team-oriented, and competent work force it is impossible to achieve a high level of service. Chapter 5 focuses on human resource issues such as staffing, training, listening, labor relations, and one's own professional growth. Someone must shelve, organize, prepare and deliver materials, maintain equipment, and staff the circulation desk. The access services positions require effective communication skills when dealing with reference, technical services, and library patrons. The staff need preparation and recognition for their important role as the eyes, ears, and hands of the library.

Facilities management, such as lighting, heating, and cooling issues, typically finds itself under the watchful eyes of access services personnel. These practical concerns of the physical environment are rarely mentioned in library classes or in the literature. Chapter 6 sheds some light on this neglected, sometimes frustrating responsibility for overseeing the physical environment that encourages patron use of the library.

Chapter 7 explores the future role and direction of access services. Access services must be proactive and not reactive to change. People who work in access services must strive for recognition as leaders in library services.

For those who want more lengthy and detailed discussion, an annotated bibliography at the back of the book offers pertinent sources on the topics considered throughout the book.

Who Should Read This Book?

This book is intended for all library professionals, because the access service function occurs in one form or another in academic, public, school, and special libraries. Whether one's library has a staff of one or twenty, maintaining access to library materials is crucial. Access services play the pivotal role in serving library patrons. Each library organizes its access services functions differently. In public libraries, access services tasks may come under the responsibility of public services. In special libraries, sometimes only one person and frequently only a very small staff may perform all the duties that in larger libraries are spread among many. School libraries may have one professional, with students as helpers. Academic libraries may have access services as a separate department, or subsumed under reference or technical services. Responsibilities vary from one library to another. The smaller the library the more varied the duties.

Each library tailors its services to accommodate the people who use it. Format, hours of service, number of volumes, volume of circulation, the nature of one's patrons, and the institutional philosophy of service are factors to investigate whenever a library undertakes any evaluation of its services. Given these considerations, creating one perfect library scenario is impossible. No two libraries may be identical, but similarities exist among access services operations.

Access services demand and have finally earned the respect of all librarians. For a variety of reasons, access services had never, up to now, been given proper credit. The perception that these services involve mundane and routine work contributes to the subject's being largely ignored in library literature. There is a tendency to use the access services department as a training ground for new librarians. While this situation provides excellent experience for new librarians, it minimizes the credibility of access services and implies that the work is not an appropriate career goal. The department is seen as one which physically disseminates information and controls library materials but not as one which performs technologically advanced functions.

Judging by discussions with other librarians and my own experience, it would seem that library schools make no substantial mention of access services in their curricula. Only circulation control is discussed in connection with automation, as part of an integrated system. By ignoring access services, the profession contributes to the misperception that they are low in status.

A common perception of circulation is that it is simple physical work and that anyone off the street can do it. Even though access services staff may not have masters' degrees in librarianship, it does not mean that they are any less professional than a librarian. Unfortunately, the staff are often treated as people low on the totem pole, or grunts.

I find the following quote entertaining: "Circulation librarians are the counterparts of commercial salesmen. Both meet the public, and upon them the organization relies for its reputation and success. The wise administrator will do well to give much attention to his salesmen."*

The library field, led by academic libraries, is slowly accepting the concept of access services as the replacement concept for circulation. The term *circulation,* however, projects a negative and limiting perception of the responsibilities of access services. In the near future, *access services* will certainly replace this term.

This book highlights the complex nature of access services and their importance to all libraries. This is the book I wanted to read when I started as access services librarian at Yale's Medical Library. The book aims to be comprehensive rather than detailed. I have attempted to show the breadth and scope of access services and their contribution to the library.

Bousfield, Humphrey G. "Circulation Systems." Library Trends 3 (Oct. 1954): 175.

1
Circulation Control

The First Encounter

Marge, access services librarian, unlocks the library doors and makes her way to the office. As Marge unlocks her office door, the staff prepare the circulation desk for the new day. Unfortunately the computer went down the night before and this morning the staff face many paper charges. At 8:10 a.m. the first patron approaches the desk, and at just that moment the phone rings. Let the day begin.

Later that day, during the weekly staff meeting, Marge asks for questions or comments. The staff look at each other but say nothing. "Oh, no," Marge thinks, but then slowly up goes Jill's hand. She begins to outline a few comments by patrons about videotapes. Parents upset about R-rated videotape titles being available for children to check out and watch at home. Patrons starting to make demands: "Get more videotapes and newer titles." "Where is your list of titles?" "Buy more copies of (any title you can think of)."

Introduction

Here is a glimpse of a library circulation control philosophy from 1893.

The charging or loan system is that part of a library's administration by which chiefly its communication with borrowers is carried on. The word loan applies to it because the books are lent, and the word charging because every library, no matter how small, with any pretence at all at having a method, has some way of keeping account of these loans.

The characteristic of a loan system best appreciated by the public is the speed with which it can receive and deliver books; and as a trifling annoyance, such as having to wait a few minutes for a book.

Another requisite is simplicity. The more complicated the system the greater the chance for error. The third thing to keep in mind is that the less the borrower's part in the operation the better he likes the system. The library must ask of him only the facts that it is absolutely necessary to have to fill his order, and if there is any *red tape* it should be kept behind the desk."*

I italicized red tape. This was written in 1893; have things changed?

Today, once patrons leave the library with materials, control over those materials is essential. What happens when someone else wants them? The function of circulation control is to locate materials that are borrowed or are not in their proper location within the library through use of either a manual or an automated record keeping system. You must be able to readily identify the location of materials.

Libraries cannot afford to give materials away or purchase unlimited copies for loan. In addition to being a routine management process, circulation records determine fines, renewals, and status. These records allow patrons and staff to know the location and availability of materials. Circulation control allows equal and efficient use of the materials. Each library—public, college, university, school, and special—has particular needs which circulation services must fulfill.

The institution, size and arrangement of collections, volume of circulation, patrons, and mission statement all influence circulation services.

---

*Plummer, Mary W. "Loan Systems." Library Journal 18 (July 1893): 242–246.

The Circulation Desk

When you enter any library, the detail that most attracts your attention is the circulation desk. The traditional library has a central circulation desk which takes care of most circulation control functions. The circulation desk is a hub of activity; patrons continuously stop by or phone for assistance or charge out materials. Service at the circulation desk is the first of many available to the patron. Libraries generally have additional service points including a reference desk, a periodical room, various departmental libraries with staff ready to give guidance, and in university libraries, a reserve desk. In addition, some libraries have branches, book drops, bookmobile service, and other specialized services.

The library patron can be a retiree, a student, a business person, an educator, a consumer, a patient, an administrator, a parent, a researcher, a child, a professional—a person from any walk of life. Some libraries serve a very broad range of patrons, while some serve only a few. Patrons are everything to the library. You must tailor all of your library's services to their needs. Here are a few questions to ask:

1. Do staff greet patrons?
2. Do staff deliver answers promptly and accurately?
3. Do staff focus in on each patron individually?
4. Do staff follow through on complaints?
5. Do staff accommodate all reasonable requests?

These questions should be asked of access services staff at the circulation desk, in the stacks, and at all other service points.

Many patrons who come into the library have a preconceived idea of a librarian, such as an introverted, shushing female. The media often portray the person sitting at the desk as an older female wearing "cat eyes" glasses with her hair in a bun, telling patrons to be quiet. Variations on this image include someone sitting with a *Be Quiet* sign on the desk, thumbing through a card catalog, or patrolling the stacks saying "shish."

Male librarians have not been excluded from this negative portrayal. This stereotype has an adverse effect on all library

The circulation desk.

staff. We must work at replacing this image with the more appropriate one of professionals working with patrons.

At the desk, materials are charged, renewed, and discharged using an automated system, a manual system, or a combination of the two. The desk must be staffed whenever the library is available to patrons for the circulation of materials. An important responsibility is scheduling coverage for the circulation desk and other critical locations. Staff at the desk must be knowledgeable about all library activities and policies, and able to explain it all from the library's perspective. Knowing why policies are established and enforced is critical in maintaining good patron relations. The projection of a friendly and helpful attitude encourages patron involvement.

One of the more difficult lessons to communicate to staff is that any reference question that cannot be answered must be referred. At times, a staff person may find it difficult to determine whether a reference question can be answered or must be referred, but with time and training he or she will find this to be less of a problem. The capability of seeing a situation from a patron's point of view is crucial to providing excellent service. Whether your circulation system is automated or manual, the same functions of charging, discharging, registering patrons, performing holds and recalls, and renewing and billing must be accomplished.

Control Systems

Manual

In public libraries the earliest recorded method of charging books for home use was by writing the author, title, and borrower's name in a day book. A real step forward was made when this daily record was transferred to a ledger to avoid searching through the day book for a single entry. Numbered pages, each one representing a borrower, were used as charge sheets. The charges were receipted by entering the date of return in a separate column.

The shortcomings of this ledger charging system, which was used until the early days of the Civil War, led to many modifications and adaptations. Manual systems moved to the dummy system, then to a temporary slip system, then to the two-card system, and to packets or envelopes for borrower, and finally to mechanical charging systems.*

The following is a description of a typical charging system from 1882:

> A person presents his card at the delivery window, and asks for a book, orally or in writing. The book, if in, is brought, its slip removed from the pocket, and the borrower's slip found in the general file. The two slips are then placed side by side, the number of each entered in the left column of the other, and the date stamped on the white slip and on the borrower's card. The borrower's own card is then put in the bookpocket, the book delivered, and the two record-slips thrown into

---

Greer, Helen. Charging Systems. *Chicago: ALA, 1955; p. 1.*

two boxes on the desk, where they remain until the closing of the
circulation department.*

Even in this age of electronics, there is nothing wrong with
using a manual circulation system. If your circulation statistics
are low, materials do not circulate, you have a small number of
patrons, or are financially unable to support automation, a well-
designed manual system of sorting and filling cards may function effectively to serve your circulation needs.

Some manual systems that had been used and in some cases
are still in use include Audio Charge System (sometimes called
dictaphone charging), Newark Charging System, Dickman Book
Charger System, Tab Charging System, Double Record Charging System, Detroit Self-Charging System, Gaylord Charging
System, and Punched Card Charging System. All of the variations of charging, past and present, attempted to achieve the
same goals. All have their advantages and disadvantages.

Manual systems range from those requiring no more than
the patron's signature and a date due stamp to those relying on
machines to assist in the charging. Manual systems offer filing
methods. In general it is wise to keep the filing as simple as
possible.

Manual system problems include labor-intensive and time-
consuming record keeping tasks, inaccuracy, high staff turnover,
difficulty in producing statistics, and lack of interface with other
library functions. When you start noticing too many errors in
records, it may be time for a new system or it may mean that it
is time to retrain staff. Whatever the reason, you will need to investigate the situation.

Past and present writings have discussed circulation systems with the two goals in mind; reducing charging and discharging time, and allowing the circulation librarian opportunities for professional growth. There have been continuous
searches for simpler, quicker, and more cost-effective circulation systems. Historically, charging systems attempted to reduce

*Linderfelt, K.A. "Charging-Systems." Library Journal 7 (June 1882): 181.

the number of routine operations required to charge and discharge materials.

Librarians have searched with the hope of achieving the perfect manual system and today the search continues for the perfect automated circulation system. There have been many innovations but the perfect system does not exist yet. Every library has different needs that its circulation system must meet.

While specific circulation policies and procedures are subject to local variation, the major component of circulation control is typically performed in a straightforward manner, which lends itself to automation. Manual circulation systems are giving way to automated circulation systems.

Automated

In an automated system, books are charged by setting the terminal to charge mode and scanning the book's barcode with a light pen. Recalls, holds, overdues, and billing notices are printed by the computer, usually on a regular batch mode schedule.

Do you need an automated system? To answer this question, first do a needs assessment. For example, a library may decide to automate its existing manual system because it cannot keep pace with its circulation growth. The needs assessment is based on a review of your existing circulation system. In addition, interviews with the staff will help you understand what really occurs with your present circulation system. You need an understanding of what is and what needs improvement. See Figure 1.1 for a checklist of possible automated circulation functions.

The decision making process includes examining library goals, the size of the circulating collection, budgetary restrictions, and the nature of support for the library. You should gather as much information as possible from other libraries, particularly libraries either nearby or of the same size. By reading literature, attending conferences, visiting other libraries, and making phone calls, you can reach the best decision. Vendors of

Figure 1.1
Circulation Functions

Establishment and Surveillance of Policies and Procedures
 Policy development
 Patron feedback analysis
 Performance analysis
Authorized Borrower Control
 Borrower registration and identification
 Special routines for exceptional borrowers
Charging Procedures
 Charging materials, books, serials, etc.
 Recording charge transaction
 Book reservation procedures
Discharging Procedures
 Discharging materials
 Recording discharge transaction
 Identification of reserved items
File Input and Maintenance (All Files)
 Transaction record
  input-charges, discharges, etc.
 Borrower file input
 Transaction control additions, deletions
 Error correction procedures
 Inventory control records
 Overdue and fine accounting
Overdue Control
 Identification of overdue items
 Receipt and control of overdues and fines
Interlibrary Loan
 Monitoring of interlibrary loan requests-incoming
 Monitoring of interlibrary loan requests-outgoing
Output Generation, Dissemination, and Reporting
 Charge records
 Overdue notices
 Reserve notices, recall notices
 Report generators
 Preparation of printed circulation and discharge lists
 Dissemination of records, reports, etc.
Reserve or Special Noncirculating Materials
 Establishment of control procedures
 Maintenance of special transaction files for noncirculating and reserve materials
 Printing of lists by course and professor
Reference Inquiry
 Identification of items on loan
 Identification of missing items
Materials Handling, Storage, and Maintenance of the Collection
 Retrieval of requested items
 Reshelving and maintenance of items
 Routing of materials
 Physical preservation of items
 Inventory of collection
 Purging of outdated and unwanted items*

*Matthews, Joseph. Choosing an Automated Library System. *Chicago: ALA,*
1980; pp. 89–90.

library-specific hardware and software are conspicuous at library conferences and you should take advantage of such opportunities to encourage demonstrations of their products.

After deciding to automate your circulation system the first step is to outline the tasks you want the system to accomplish. Your needs assessment will also assist you as you investigate automated circulation systems.

An automated circulation control system should:

1. Be available whenever the library is open, running continuously; there should be no scheduled down time;
2. Charge: the system should link authorized borrower, book and date due together fast and correctly, and indicate date due and let staff know patron identity;
3. Determine location of an item rapidly;
4. Identify, hold and recall items;
5. Prepare overdue notices;
6. Prepare lists of items out on loan to any borrower and check for excessive numbers of books checked out;
7. Detect delinquent borrowers at time of check out;
8. Discharge: the system should update returned materials in files and forgive or add fines to account; and
9. Prepare management information such as statistics and reports

and it should do them reliably and economically. Additional features would include the system's

1. Registering patrons and adding data to the data base;
2. Handling a number of different due dates;
3. Permitting renewal of books;
4. Indicating, calculating and accounting for fines;
5. Providing search capabilities;
6. Displaying status of item, number of copies and whether it or they are checked out;
7. Permitting communication between terminals;
8. Blocking excessive borrowing; and
9. Interfacing with other library functions.*

Matthews, Joseph, p.88.

It is interesting that the following are the same sort of questions that were asked for the examination of various charging systems in 1893.

1. Is a given book out?
2. If out who has it?
3. When did he take it?
4. When is it to be sent for, as overdue?
5. Has the book ever been out?
6. How many and what books are now out, charged to borrowers?
7. Has a given person a book charged to him? How many books? What books?
8. Is the person's card still in force and used?
9. Has this person a right to draw books?*

When selecting a system, numerous options are available. Will you purchase a vendor turnkey system or software, develop an in-house system, or modify an existing system?

Traditionally, libraries have invested in the turnkey automation solution. The turnkey solution is analogous to the operation of a car wherein the consumer simply gets in and "turns the key," not knowing or caring how the car operates or is designed. Similarly, libraries have traditionally attempted to install automated systems that have allowed them to "turn on the system" without having any experienced technical or programming personnel on staff.† Software vendors only guarantee that the software is free of defect.

Medium-sized and larger public and academic libraries have relied on both mainframe-based and minicomputer-based products. Examples of IBM mainframes include NOTIS and IBM's own DOBIS/LIBIS program. Minicomputer-based turnkey circulation control systems are available from CLSI, Geac, Data Research Associates (DRA), and Dynix.

---

*Plummer, Mary W., p. 243.

†Walton, Robert A., and Bridge, Frank R. "Automated System Marketplace 1990: Focusing on Software Sales and Joint Ventures." Library Journal 115, 6 (1990): 58.

Reasonably priced and designed for readily available hardware configurations, microcomputer-based circulation control programs have proven popular with small public, school, and special libraries. Vendors include Follett, Gaylord, Easy Data, Data Trek, and Richmond Software.*

Some additional steps to take: talk to colleagues at similar libraries; involve all levels of the department in the decision; seek technical advice from the inside and the outside; and finally do not trust one vendor to do it all.

Once a year the *Library Systems Newsletter,* published by Library Technology Reports, surveys automated library system vendors. The issue is devoted to the vendors which offer integrated, multiuser, multifunction systems. The vendor reports are arranged alphabetically and based on information provided by the respondents.

The March 1990 issue surveyed 25 companies. Seventeen offered both turnkey and software packages, five offered software only, and three offered only turnkey systems. The 25 respondents sold 435 systems during 1989 as compared with 376 in 1988, 350 in 1978, 210 in 1986, 196 in 1985, and 232 in 1984.†

During 1989, CLSI continued its dominant position as leader in worldwide installations. It also reversed the trend of prior years and increased the numbers of its installations in public libraries. With 345, CLSI led all vendors in numbers of installed and accepted systems; Dynix was second, with 343; Geac third (177); and IBM's DOBIS was fourth (167). Although Dynix did not capture first place, it posted a large increase in academic installations, primarily in community colleges. Dynix maintained its position as clearly the favorite vendor of public libraries. Dynix reported the highest number during 1989 of new system sales: 117.

---

*Saffady, William. "Library Automation." Library Trends 37, 3 (1989): 272.

†"Annual Survey of Automated Library System Vendors." Library Systems Newsletter 10, 3 (1990).

The CLSI offer is for turnkey systems only. As of 1989, all of its sites had both circulation and local cataloging. Dynix offers turnkey and software. During 1989, 95 percent of Dynix sites used its circulation function. Geac offers turnkey using its own hardware, operating system, and programming language. Ninety-seven percent of Geac's sites use its circulation function.

Turnkey Systems

In the turnkey environment, the vendor selects a hardware platform, develops the software, and sells the system's package to the library with the related installation, training, and maintenance services that are necessary to make the project a success.*

Turnkey systems can, with few changes, be used for circulation control. You save money on research costs, development and programming costs but all the control of the program by which the system can be modified is in the hands of the vendor.

Libraries choose to purchase a turnkey system rather than develop their own systems for several reasons. The cost of purchase is less than the cost of development; libraries expect that their own local system would be too complicated; the development of a local system requires considerable staffing resources; and acceptable turnkey systems already exist.

Software Vendors

Marketplace activity in 1989 demonstrated that software-only sales are increasing in popularity. Academic libraries are interested in having their automated library systems be interactive partners on campus-wide computing networks. Public libraries want to link their systems with others' for enhanced resource sharing and to incorporate public "information-oriented" ser-

---

*Walton, Robert A., p. 58.

vices such as specialized databases and community electronic bulletin boards. The marketplace, however, changes from year to year.*

Innovative Corporation was the big surprise of 1989, capturing the lead position in academic libraries both in worldwide and United States installations. Once thought of as a specialist, technical services vendor Innovative has now pushed NOTIS to second place in total systems installed and passed NOTIS, Dynix, IBM, and DRA in academic installations during 1989.

The realities of academic demographics have caused NOTIS to suffer. Many of the large Association of Research Libraries institutions have already automated with NOTIS or gone in another direction. This system appeals primarily to the largest library institutions, those capable of operating a large IBM mainframe computer. The vendors of NOTIS have now initiated an aggressive transition to a medium-sized IBM platform and will begin marketing it to the medium-sized academic library market.†

Unfortunately the literature does not address the automation needs of the small public or school library.

> Library literature teems with articles pertaining to large library automation, i.e. libraries where there are directors, task forces, and staff large enough to support such an undertaking. What seems to be lacking is published information on the perils and pitfalls of small library automation, small library being defined as having collections containing fewer than 35,000 volumes and a professional staff of three or less. Although the professionals in small libraries face the identical problems of their counterparts in large libraries, they have neither the staff nor the financial support to follow published advice. Thus, many small libraries are hindered in their efforts to automate services.§

---

*Walton, Robert A., p. 58.

†*Walton, Robert A., p. 61.*

§*Gaudet, Jean Ann. "Automating the Circulation Services of a Small Library."* Library Resources and Technical Services *31, 3 (1987): 249.*

Now that you have addressed what system you will be using, one of your next important steps is the barcoding of your collection.

Barcoding

What are barcodes? Barcodes are a series of printed lines and spaces of varying widths which represent numbers, symbols or letters of the alphabet.

Barcoding is often one of the first critical projects a library faces during the process of automating circulation. There are two types of barcodes—smart and dumb. (See Figure 1.2 for examples.) Barcodes that are prematched to bibliographic item records are smart. The computer assigns a unique barcode number to each item in the collection during database processing. Then during barcode label production, the computers associate the appropriate call number and copy number with each barcode. The barcodes are arranged by call number for ease of application. These smart barcodes are for specific items in the collection. Usually smart barcodes are applied prior to bringing up circulation.

Barcoding specifications are time-consuming to write, but important for the project. Your system must be able to "read" the barcode. Various formats have been established for the representation of the data. Their specifications allow for capture, and provide for verification in the scanning process.*

You might consider using piggyback barcodes because they can be removed before they are to be attached permanently; they are reusable.

Before undertaking the barcoding, consider a preliminary shelf reading of the collection. Accurate shelf arrangement is a tremendous asset when it comes time to attach the barcodes to the materials.

The barcoding of a library's collection can go quickly if you are prepared and have plenty of help. Ask for volunteers, hire additional staff, involve local high school or college students, or

---

*Rahn, Erwin. "Bar Codes for Libraries." Library Hi Tech 6 (1988): 73–77.

Figure 1.2
Sample Barcodes

Smart Barcode:

    Line 1 : Library name
    Line 2 : Specific library
             location (e.g. GEO,
             REF)
    Line 3 : Call number
    Line 4 : Brief Title information
    Line 5 : 14-digit Item ID

Dumb Barcode:

    Line 1 : Library name
    Line 2 : 14-digit Item ID

barcode during slow periods of use. You may decide to provide special motivators or incentives, such as T-shirts saying "I survived the barcoding at...," coffee and doughnuts, or a pizza party for your helpers.

During the smart barcoding you will need to complete a report for each problem (see Figure 1.3).

You can now work on clearing up these problems.

In the case of smart barcodes, pilot testing is another option. A sample list of barcode data can be generated well in advance. Your staff can run the list through the various steps. This allows you to preview possible problems, assess the quality of barcode production, and experiment with procedures.

Dumb barcodes are manually linked to the database item records. Unlike smart barcodes, dumb barcodes are applied at random with no need to match, but at some point must be linked to the item records at the individual level in the database. Often item records are created during the linking process.

The decision to use smart or dumb barcodes is usually based on the financial situation, time considerations, or staffing constraints; neither approach, of course, is error free.

Figure 1.3
Barcoding Problem Report

Call Number _____
Title _____

Not on shelf _____
Multi-volumes, 1 barcode _____
Multi-barcodes, 1 volume _____
Lost Book Marker _____
No barcode _____
Other problem _____
Applied barcode by mistake _____

Another decision is the location of the barcode on the materials. Inside front or back cover, on front or back cover, or on both are all possible. Even nonprint items should be barcoded. Libraries tend to apply barcodes at the point of receipt, in cataloging, or at the moment of spine labeling.

Regardless of the use of smart barcodes initially, libraries frequently switch to dumb barcodes for new additions to the collection. You must establish procedures for the barcoding of new materials and as binding and repair necessitate replacement.

During daily circulation operation, books without barcodes will be brought to the circulation desk for charging. The steps to this procedure include searching the database, finding the record, and linking it. If no record is found, then you must create a brief skeleton record before the material circulates and it is linked. Most systems allow you to flag the record to update it when the book returns and is discharged. You could also stamp the book in such a way as to signify a need to update.

Flow charts and pictorial representations help describe and communicate, in broad terms, the circulation function. For an example of processing books without barcodes, see Figure 1.4.

Figure 1.4

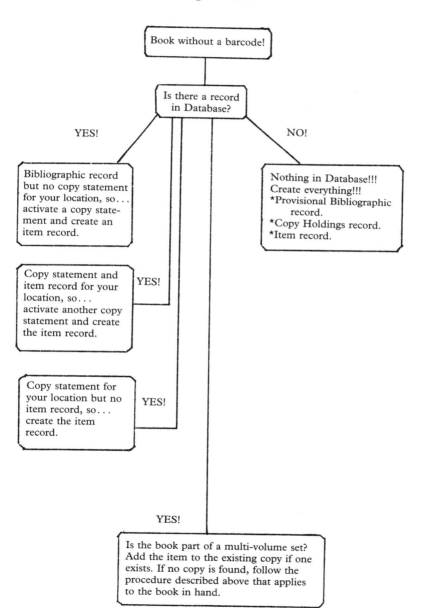

Figure 1.5
For Items Not Already Barcoded
Backup Charge

```
                                          ┌─────────────────
                                          │  Entered by
                                          │
        CALL #:_____

        AUTHOR:_____

        _____

        TITLE:_____
```

INITIALS:		
BARCODE:		DATE DUE:
NOTE:	MATERIAL TYPE:	LOCATION:

```
        PATRON NAME:_____

        ID #:_____   PHONE #:_____
```

You also need a procedure to charge out materials should the circulation system be unavailable. In such cases there are two alternative procedures you may follow: you may use a double barcode system, in which one places a barcode in the book and an identical barcode on a paper form (see Figure 1.5), or you may write down information on a paper charge form. Both procedures allow for the entry of data into the computer after materials have been charged out.

Implementation and the Future

The implementation phase is stressful, causing feelings of fear and self-doubt. People begin to wonder what will happen if they cannot do the job, and indeed some of the staff may not be able to perform their new tasks. A full orientation and training program is necessary. A positive attitude helps people deal with the change, learn with less stress, and incorporate helpful feelings into work patterns.

Probably the biggest impact that automation has on circulation control is its influence on policies, procedures, and work flow. It is possible for branch libraries to standardize policies. Issues such as placement of the terminal and sufficient work space will need careful examination. Every library will have its own requirements.

With any project, savings is the goal. With automation, long term savings is the goal. Savings are not immediate because of hidden costs, such as initial slow production, backlog, training, and cost of equipment and hardware. Future costs to consider include those that result from an upgrade of the system and new demands for services as a result of automation. New services, such as document delivery, may become a necessity—especially with an online catalog, because patrons have access to more information.

Another potentially painful future decision will come from the need to replace one automated circulation system with another.

This could happen for a number of reasons: (1) A library may abandon a stand-alone function for an integrated system; for example, knowledge of the availability of materials in the public catalog is as important as knowing what the library owns. (2) The needs of the library may grow or change. (3) A new product may achieve the same results in a more efficient way. (4) The hardware required may no longer be available or serviceable. (5) The vendor has gone out of business or has dropped the product. As a consequence of any of these events a library may change its automated system two or three times.

With hardware in place, software checked, procedures finalized, barcodes applied, documentation written, and system operational, your next step, training, is the most important.

Training

Whether you use a manual or an automated circulation system, the desk staff requires training. Training of staff is crucial to the success of circulation control. Unfortunately, many libraries give it too little attention. They expect staff to learn policies and procedures by oral instruction and observation.

You must make a full commitment of time and money to training. There is no substitute for this. When you consider the amount of time that is needed to keep a library running, sometimes 12 or more hours a day, staff training takes on even more importance. Materials charged out at 8:30 p.m. require the same strict procedure as when they are charged out at 8:30 a.m.

Written up-to-date procedures are very important, particularly during early morning or late evening hours. Staff can refer to a manual instead of calling you at home for an answer to a simple question. You want the staff to gain a sense of responsibility and build their confidence.

When you are automating circulation or switching to a new system, training becomes the key to the success of the project. Who will do the training? When researching possible automated systems it is important to consider the training component of the vendor. Carefully evaluate the training set-up proposed by the vendor to make certain it will work for your library. Vendors typically train the trainers. When the vendor's part of the training is over, what next?

You want the best trainers possible from your staff. They may or may not be your supervisors. One way to get the best trainers is to do an anonymous survey of all staff. Trainers must transcend the organizational chart, and political pressures of the library.

Everyone must be trained but not everyone needs the same level of training. Supervisors need to know everything, while a student at the circulation desk only needs to know how to charge or discharge materials, and place a hold or recall. Fines, blocks, and other complex transactions will probably not be performed by students or volunteers.

Figure 1.6

CIRCULATION DESK   NAME
TRAINING CHECK LIST   DATE

Date and initial each section, when training has been completed

CHARGE/RENEW
Manual _____
GEAC _____
W/Barcode _____

DISCHARGE
Manual _____
GEAC _____
Hold/Recall _____

INQUIRY
GEAC _____
Orbis _____
Bindery _____
Patron _____

COPY CARDS
Sell-cash _____
Charge
Re-encode _____

TELEPHONE
Etiquette _____
Closing _____
Message _____

PRIVILEGES
Information _____
Form _____
Input _____

OVERDUE
Fines _____
BFR _____
Proc Fee _____
Bursar _____
Notices _____

NEW MATERIALS
Barcode _____
Input _____
New Shelf _____
Holds _____
Jour Res _____

SHELVING
Reserve _____
Journ Res _____
Thesis _____

PROBLEM PATRON
Role Play _____
Handout

Individuals learn at varying speeds. This will be discussed further in Chapter 5. Training for daily tasks is more important than anything else.

Use of a training check list is one way to monitor and record the training progress of staff (see Figure 1.6). A manual and step-by-step instructions are just two training necessities. Inaccuracy in procedures and duties can cause confusion and lead to loss of materials. Let new staff observe, first, then slowly work them into the desk, while all the time encouraging questions.

Materials

What materials are in your library? The patrons, library programs and philosophy of service determine the subject matter and scope of materials in the library. If your clientele are elementary school children, then you do not collect Fortune 500 annual reports. Likewise a corporate library would not include children's literature. Collection development decides what materials make up the library's collections. Art prints, paperbacks, dissertations, computers, filmstrips, kits, maps and charts, microform, motion pictures, pamphlets, periodicals, photographs, models, plants, live animals, compact discs, records, newspapers, laser discs, hardcover, fiction, textbooks, videotapes, software, globes, or toys can all circulate. A library may provide and circulate any format.

Today nonprint items are becoming as common as books in libraries. Exactly what is a nonprint item? (1) The item must appeal to the sight or hearing of the library patron. (2) Under normal conditions, the item requires additional equipment for use. (3) The printed word must not represent the essence of the medium.* Nonprint materials include videotapes, audiotapes, models, laser discs, and toys.

One stumbling block to the development of nonprint col-

---

*Wall, Thomas B. "Nonprint Materials: A Definition and Some Practical Considerations on Their Maintenance." Library Trends 34, 1 (1985): 131.

lections is the perception that the materials are so expensive compared with books that they must require special security measures. The consequences include the creation of segregated locations, expensive packaging, restrictive circulation policies and the excessive use of staff time to facilitate control of the materials. In fact, the average prices of videos and compact discs have dropped sharply, and now in some cases cost less than books.

Nonprint materials have been slow to gain full acceptance from some academics. In academic libraries the book is seen as the only medium for research. Nonprint materials requiring machines encounter even more resistance.

Nonprint materials can impact print materials. Libraries presently circulating videotapes note an increase in requests for the literature and for any adaptations. The opposite may also occur when patrons may watch the video instead of reading the book.*

If you have materials requiring equipment, does the library provide the necessary equipment and if so, who will be responsible for its operation and maintenance? Most media are dependent upon specialized equipment, which, if not properly maintained, causes serious damage to the materials. Every piece of equipment requires some maintenance. One thing to keep in mind when selecting equipment is whether maintenance can be done by staff, by a representative of the company that sells it, or by a third party. There is no such thing as maintenance-free equipment.

Let us take a look at how the format of the material influences a library.

Microform

The term microform describes any form of microreproduction. It has the obvious advantages of taking up less space than publications on paper, being less expensive to purchase and

---

This information was stated in a number of articles.

lasting longer than paper. You may decide that it is feasible to retain periodicals in both microfiche and bound form. The microform would be helpful when materials are at the bindery, or in the case of high use titles.

Materials in microform include historical books and journals in danger of deterioration, many bibliographies, catalogs and journals. Almost all paper information can be microfilmed, thus reducing storage space. This is cheaper than maintaining paper copies considering the costs of binding and preserving. When deciding what to microfilm, important considerations include the nature of the information (does the reader need to refer to other pages of the same source), frequency of use, and cost. The overwhelming consideration is the patron. The masters must be stored in a secured space.

Microfilm is a continuous strip of film with no fixed length. Microfiche is a rectangular piece of film. Neither film nor fiche can be read without the use of special equipment, which magnifies the image so that it becomes legible.

Microform readers allow film to be wound at a high speed. There is usually a slower winding facility or a manual control which can be used to find the precise frame.

Microfiche is placed between two sheets of glass and inserted into the machine above the light source. Microfiche readers are small, easy to use and maintain, and are relatively inexpensive. Since there are fewer moving parts than microfilm readers, they are easier to use and suffer fewer mechanical problems.

Whether film or fiche is used, the image on the screen is normally easy to read, although it is sometimes necessary to adjust the focus to obtain clarity and definition.

The lack of good equipment and space can discourage use of microforms. People tend to resist microform, because they believe it to be difficult to read with poor images, and they are confined to a machine. Even the best equipment can cause eyestrain after prolonged viewing, and of course film and fiche are not as convenient to browse through as books.

Staff must assist patrons with the reading equipment and

ensure that the equipment works and is maintained regularly. Staff must be well acquainted with the operation of the readers and printers. You need well-trained staff with positive attitudes toward the equipment. Staff may hate microform as much as patrons but must actively minimize the inconveniences of the units.

You should purchase the best reading and copying equipment. A supply of frequently used lamps and parts should be kept on hand. The microform reading area needs to be organized, well lighted, and well maintained. If microforms circulate, you may decide to supply portable microfiche readers for home use.

Newspapers are a prime example of material that undoubtedly will be microfilmed. Newspapers are physically difficult to handle, bulky, and fragile. Newspapers published since 1880 on highly acidic wood pulp disintegrate rapidly, creating the need for extensive microfilming programs to preserve them.

Microfilming has come to be regarded as the most practical preservation technique now available. It has helped libraries withdraw issues in bad shape and reduce the bulk of collections.[*]

Currently, microfilm is the most useful and most widely used technology for the preservation of newspapers. Someday laser disc technology may supplant microfilm in its role in preservation.

Summary

School libraries have toys or games for rainy day activities and audiovisual equipment for everyday classroom use. Public libraries have a wide variety of materials for their diverse audience. Special libraries cater to patrons' specific needs. For example, bank libraries may include corporate annual reports, business reference materials, and software. Hospital library

---

[*] *Upham, Lois N.* Newspapers in the Library: New Approaches to Management and Reference Work. *New York: Haworth Press, 1988; p. 2*

collections generally include medical, consumer health, and in some cases fiction materials for patients. Academic libraries support the curriculum of their institutions and research activities. No matter what the material, you need control over it. The intended use of the collection generally determines whether it circulates.

Collections

Circulating

No matter what the material, if it leaves the library you must control it. Here is where your manual or automated system really comes into play. Policies and procedures must be clearly explained.

Circulating collections include both print and nonprint materials. Special containers, boxes, cases, or trays may be necessary to protect circulating nonprint materials.

Every library will have special issues to consider in circulating materials. For example, film and video libraries may need a scheduling system which maintains a calendar of future booking shipments, or a sign-up list. Those libraries that circulate software generally circulate backup copies of software programs and keep the originals in protective containers.

Academic libraries often charge materials to carrels for long term use. In this case you must maintain schedules for reservations and renewing or clearing out materials, and systems to label or lock carrels when not in use.

Whatever materials circulate they must be consistently controlled. Patrons need to know if the material is available for their use.

Reserve

Reserve collections in academic libraries involve materials that are set aside from the regular collection and designated either for special purposes, such as assigned student readings, or as heavy-use materials. Sometimes the nature of the materials themselves cause them to be in a reserve collection. Loan periods are short term: one or two hours, overnight, or possibly one day on a second copy. You may establish heavy fine schedules for late returns. A waiting list for heavily requested copies may need to be maintained if additional copies cannot be purchased. Materials may be housed in an open reserve area, a closed reserve area, or a reserve reading room.

Some method of indicating materials on reserve is necessary. Methods used include overlays or markers in catalog, location in online catalog, shelf dummies, charge card in circulation file, temporary card file at desk or in catalog, colored stickers or reserve labels on books. Patrons must know the location, permanent or temporary, of the materials.

There are different ways to arrange the materials. They may be shelved by call numbers, which gives subject arrangement; by course, which requires dummies for referral of books on reserve for more than one course; or by author or title. Staff that work with reserve collections will become familiar with the titles and with such characterizations as "the big red book." Photocopies can be filed alphabetically by author of article, by course number or instructor's name. All items for a particular course can be bound together and treated as book material.

When materials are for classes, reminders for reading lists and recommendations for purchases must be sent out to instructors prior to each quarter or semester (see Figures 1.7 and 1.8).

The materials may go into the general collection and circulate. In public libraries, the term reserve refers to the holding of a specific title in a patron's name for a period of time.

Reference

Reference materials that never leave the library include phone books, dictionaries, atlases, handbooks, indexes and abstracts, almanacs, and directories. Such materials are intended for quick information and for use by staff and patrons.

Figure 1.7
Academic Library
Reserve Request

ALL RESERVE PHOTOCOPY loans and requests must be submitted on this library form.

Please Complete a Separate Form for Each Item.   Date _____

PLEASE PRINT CLEARLY.

PERIODICAL _____

VOLUME _____ ISSUE_____ DATE _____

AUTHOR _____

TITLE OF ARTICLE _____

_____

INCLUSIVE PAGINATION _____

I lend / request these photocopies for course reserve in compliance with the Copyright Law.

NOTICE

ORDER

WARNING CONCERNING COPYRIGHT RESTRICTIONS

The copyright law of the United States (title 17, United States Code) governs the making of photocopies or other reproductions of copyright material.

Under certain conditions specified in the law, libraries and archives are authorized to furnish a photocopy or other reproduction. One of these specified conditions is that the photocopy or reproduction is not to be "used for any purpose other than private study, scholarship, or research." If a user makes a request for, or later uses, a photocopy or reproduction for purposes in excess of "fair use," that user may be liable for copyright infringement.

This institution reserves the right to refuse to accept a copying order, if in its judgment, fulfillment of the order would involve violation of copyright law.

The library adheres to the following guidelines: 1. One copy of an article; 2. No more than 50 pages of an article; 3. Only one article per issue of chapter; 4. No more than 3 articles per volume.

One copy of an article may be made by the faculty member. This copy must have "Property of Dr. *(faculty member's last name)*." written on the front page of the article.

One additional copy of an article may be made by the library staff.

The only exception to this 2-copy policy is in cases where the faculty member receives written permission from the publisher to make multiple copies of a particular article.

Name: _____   Status and Dept.: _____

Address: _____   Telephone: _____

Course: _____   Term: _____ Year: _____

No. of sheets: _____   _____

Figure 1.8

RESERVE BOOK LIST

Course No. & Title: _____ Number of Students: _____

Instructor: _____ Extension: _____

Dates needed on reserve—specify last day needed

☐ All terms _____ ☐ Fall term _____ ☐ Spring term _____
           until   until   until

                      ☐ Winter term _____ ☐ Summer term _____
                               until   until

☐ Other (specify): _____
                    from   —   until

Please list titles alphabetically by author, one book in each space.

Call Number	Author (last name, first name)	Complete title, edition (if applicable), and date

Reference materials are usually shelved on open stacks allowing patrons and staff the opportunity to consult the holdings freely. They may be arranged by type of material—directories or dictionaries, for instance—or by subject. The materials need frequent and accurate shelving. Older editions may circulate eventually.

Special Collections

Some materials are fragile, invaluable, not cataloged, and meant never to leave the library. Archives, historical papers, correspondence, papers and manuscripts, drawings, paintings or photographs may have restrictive use. Materials may be in storage and unorganized and therefore difficult to secure. Access to special collections tends to be limited.

New Materials

What do you do with recently received materials? Newly cataloged materials should remain on a "new book" shelf for all patrons to see. You will need to notify patrons when new materials are ready to circulate and establish sign up procedures and loan periods. If more than one patron requests the material, you will need to place holds and recalls on the material.

Another issue, when you have an integrated automated system, is whether to circulate materials that have not been cataloged. Patrons will know when a book is newly received or being processed. Will you catalog it immediately if requested or circulate uncataloged? Both methods require procedures to be clearly stated.

Policies and Procedures

Marge and the Videos

Marge's library received a gift of $15,000 to start a videotape collection. Marge thought the actual process of circulating videos should be no more complicated than circulating other items; however she discovered that she needed to establish several new policies and procedures:

- Limits on loan time and number of videos per patron per period.
- Age limitations (if any) for use of collection, or any part of collection.
- Registration/responsibility card for video users or for minors' parents to sign.
- Overdue fines—cost per day or per hour.
- Replacement/damage policy—sliding discount scale based upon use or current replacement cost and repair cost.
- Overdue penalty—a suspension of service after so many overdues within a certain time period.
- Circulation fees or handling charges.*

Marge decides on a few policies quickly: periods should be established for equitable use, and a two-tier circulation period— three days for features, one week for nonfiction—should be in effect.

Policies are general guidelines which set boundaries, while procedures are step-by-step recipes which carry out policies. Workable policy statements that guide staff in procedures when dealing with services, including hours, privileges, interlibrary loans, fines, lost books, loan periods, and other services, should be set by "you." Rules are established procedures. The staff need to know why policies exist, to explain to patrons when necessary.

Post a set of library rules and policies or make policies available to patrons. Also, periodically publish circulation policies in your library newsletter. Staff must keep accurate, up-to-date records and follow all policies and procedures or chaos will reign.

---

*Scholtz, James C. Developing and Maintaining Video Collections in Libraries. Santa Barbara: ABC-Clio, 1989; p. 66.

Privileges

Library cards may be issued to each patron who intends to borrow or use library materials. This area opens up a whole realm of questions that need resolving by establishing policies.

In the case of children, parents may be asked to sign a statement taking responsibility for the materials checked out by their child. Such a statement makes the parent responsible for loss or damage of materials.

Should parents limit their own children's borrowing privileges by signing a form stating that the youngster may not borrow from adult materials? Should children obtain library cards only with the signature of a parent or guardian?

How do people apply for privileges? (See Figure 1.9.)

What about visitors? Should there be policies limiting the number of items charged out? What about access to other services? Are all services available?

Issues that require the setting of policies include deciding who can take out materials; will you issue cards or use existing ID; who can use what and for how long; do you establish different loan periods for classes of patrons; and do you fine everybody. Should delinquent borrowers' library privileges be suspended? Borrowing privileges may be denied but what about other privileges?

Loan Periods

A review of policies on loan periods from a survey of 203 public libraries, done over a hundred years ago in 1889, yielded the following interesting data—interesting because the situations is very similar today.

In 132 libraries the loan period was 14 days for all works issued. Other libraries made distinctions between magazines and books, or new books and older ones, or according to number of volumes and size of work, or between juvenile and adult readers, or city and county borrowers, and hence varied their loan periods accordingly. In 43 libraries the periods were 7 and

Figure 1.9
PRIVILEGES APPLICATION

Must have valid identification.

Name _____
         Last   First   Initial

Social Security Number _____-_____-_____

*Home Address _____
                        Street

         _____
         City   State   Zip
    Phone ( )_____

*Business Address _____
                        Name of Company

         _____
         Street or Building and Number

         _____
         City   State   Zip
    Phone ( )_____ Ext. _____

14 days; in 3 libraries the periods were 7, 14, and 28 days; and in 4 libraries the periods were 14 and 21 days. Nearly all of the libraries allowed one or more renewals or reissues of the book to the same person. Twenty did not renew new books.*

In one-person libraries (of the present-day), it is best to keep circulation procedures simple. Allow patrons enough time so that you do not constantly have to send overdue notices. As long as there is a way to recall materials, a long loan period is not a factor. If the proper records are kept there should be no complications. Some libraries may establish self-service procedures for patrons such as special keys for library access and self-chargeout of materials after regular business hours.

*Carr, H.J. *"Report on Charging Systems."* Library Journal *14 (May–June, 1889): 210–211.*

Heavily used or hard to control items should not circulate. Journals may circulate for two hours for copying purposes. Many offices have their own equipment to copy.

Loan periods should be based on the type of material. If the material is in little demand and if other materials covering the same subject are available, it may be given a long-term period, which can range from one week to a year. Heavy-use items should be given a very short-term period, which is usually one hour, two hours, or overnight. Are renewals allowed? How many—a limited or an indefinite number?

The location of a library may be a factor in setting policy. Should there be special privileges for area residents? Do patrons travel long distances? If so, longer loan periods may be necessary. In such cases, phone renewals or mail returns may also be acceptable.

What happens when patrons are on vacation? One possibility is the use of padded preaddressed mailers. For example, patrons could return audio tapes after being used. You would probably have patrons accrue fines, and be charged replacement costs for tapes lost or damaged in the mail.

Interlibrary loan circulation loan periods may be longer than usual because of mailing time.

Should videotapes be physically examined upon their return: To be assured that the case and cassette match before the mix up becomes untraceable? To rewind? To evaluate the condition of the item and to make sure the video is in working order and to visually inspect for any breaks, cracks, or excessive rattles?

There are various viewpoints on nonprint materials. Some people advocate not varying the loan periods because it is confusing to patrons. Others feel that different materials do require different loan periods. There is also the consideration that if you do not check the condition of each book on its return, it is inconsistent to check each nonprint item. You might still, however, check kits and expensive items.

The size of the library may influence the flexibility of your policies. Is there close daily contact with patrons? Is it hard to keep track of patrons and to know them? The more personal contact you have with the patrons, the more you will be accommodating to their needs.

Overdues

Overdues are problems for any library. An overdue book is a serious problem only when another patron is denied access to that title. Will you have an overdue penalty? For instance, would you suspend services after so many overdues within a specific time frame?

Overdue notices can be sent immediately or several days or weeks after due date. Other issues to consider: how many notices should be sent? Are notices strictly reminders? If you do not send notices, is the patron still liable? If the patron does not receive a notice, is it his or her responsibility to notify the library of address changes?

In any case, remind the patron that it is his or her responsibility to check the due date. Moreover, keep track of all correspondences.

A record of the number of overdue notices sent to patrons can help determine if the loan period is too short or too long. A higher percentage of overdues as compared to circulation indicates a possible need to increase the loan period.

Renewals

Should the library accept phone or mail renewals? Or should it accept only in-person renewals? Renewals are a way of extending loan periods for patrons (see Figure 1.10). Placing a hold on an item is one way of increasing the accessibility of materials. If a book requested by a patron is in circulation, a hold can be put on the book to ensure that the book is not renewed and is held for the requestor. A time is set within which the patron must pick up the item.

Figure 1.10

```
                    ┌─────────────────┐
                    │    RENEWAL      │
                    └─────────────────┘
   (Name)_____

   ID No._____

   ┌──────────────────────────────────────────────┐
   │ Call No.                                       │
   │              ║   ─────────────────────────     │
   │              ║   Barcode No.                    │
   │              ║   ─────────────────────────     │
   │                  Old Due Date                   │
   └──────────────────────────────────────────────┘
   ┌──────────────────────────────────────────────┐
   │ Call No.                                       │
   │              ║   ─────────────────────────     │
   │              ║   Barcode No.                    │
   │              ║   ─────────────────────────     │
   │                  Old Due Date                   │
   └──────────────────────────────────────────────┘
```

Figure 1.11

```
            ┌──────────────────────────────────┐
            │   COMPUTER RECALL / HOLD         │
            └──────────────────────────────────┘
       ┌──────────────────────────────────────────┐
       │  Call Number                              │
       │                                           │
       │                                           │
       │  ───────────────────────────────────      │
       │  Title                                    │
       └──────────────────────────────────────────┘
                     ┌──────────────┐
                     │ HOLD/RECALL FOR │
       ┌─────────────┴──────────────┴─────────────┐
       │  ───────────────────────────────────      │
       │  Name                                     │
       │  ───────────────────────────────────      │
       │  ID No.                                   │
       │                                           │
       │  ───────────────────────────────────      │
       │  Address                                  │
       │  ───────────────────────────────────      │
       │                                           │
       │  ───────────────────────────────────      │
       │  Phone                                    │
       └──────────────────────────────────────────┘
       ┌──────────────────────────────────────────┐
       │                                           │
       │  ───────────────────────────────────      │
       │  Pick-up Location                         │
       │  Date due for Recall_____       │
       └──────────────────────────────────────────┘
```

Recalls and Holds

Can materials be recalled? (See Figure 1.11.) Recalls involve items that have not been out for their full loan period. Many libraries state that the material is subject to recall after two weeks. Patrons must return material when it has been recalled. Usually a high fine is charged for late returns of recalls. Rush recalls are usually reserved for reserve materials.

Holds are available for those patrons who do not mind waiting for the material to return to the library. Such patrons are put on a waiting list.

Fines

Back in 1889, fines were imposed to protect the library against loss and "to secure to all a just and equitable share in its benefits. Any person detaining a book longer than the regulations permit, shall be fined . . . for each day of such retention." In 10 libraries a fine of 1 cent per day was assessed; in 106 libraries, 2 cents per day; in 18, 3 cents; in 20, 5 cents; and in 2, 10 cents per day. In yet others, the rate increased for certain intervals over time.*

Today, rates, amounts and types of fines vary from one library to another. Fines should be set at rates that are standard for your area and type of library. Do not set your fines so high that they work against the return to the library: "I owe so much, I might as well keep it." High charges have been known to both discourage use and be an incentive to return materials on time. Low charges may not be worth the cost and the effort to collect and may not discourage abusers; but low charges may also not deter library use.

Charging fines should be considered a method of getting the prompt return of materials to the library, not as a source of income.

Fine policy should be posted in an obvious place. Do you

*Carr, H.J., p. 211.

Figure 1.12

```
┌─────────────────────────────────────────────────────┐
│              REQUEST FOR FINE WAIVER                  │
│                                                       │
│   NAME:_____        │
│                                                       │
│   I.D. NO.:_____        │
│                                                       │
│   PHONE:_____        │
│                                                       │
│   TYPE OF FINE:                                       │
│                                                       │
│                    OVERDUE_____                     │
│                                                       │
│                    RECALL _____                     │
│                                                       │
│   CALL NUMBER:                                        │
│                                                       │
│   REASON FOR WAIVER:                                  │
│                                                       │
│                                                       │
│                                   _____         │
│                                   INITIALS            │
└─────────────────────────────────────────────────────┘
```

add a processing charge to the amount charged for lost or ruined materials?

Whom do you fine, waive or forgive? (See Figure 1.12.) Do you accept cash or charge? Any grace period? How far will you go to collect the fines: Send notices? Go to a collection agency? Notify the police? Another means to accomplish the goal of returning materials is to create a Forgiveness of Fines Month. During a given month forgive all fines, no matter how great, on all returned materials.

Hours

The number of hours it stays open are dictated by a library's budget. The scheduling of staff is an extremely important duty but a potential source of frustration, especially when you consider the long hours needed to be filled. How far geographically are your patrons from the library? How do you let people know that the library is closing earlier than normal?

An answering machine providing information, such as hours, can be quite helpful to patrons and staff.

Statistics

Circulation statistics are a reflection of the kind of service provided to patrons. Is the library open a sufficient and convenient number of hours? Do you provide excellent service? Does the collection reflect your patron needs? Are new materials provided and displayed? If you can answer these questions mostly in the affirmative, the results will be a high degree of use of your library. For example, public libraries consider how their communities are being served. You may decide to circulate videocassettes, paperbacks, or non–English-language materials, or even to shelve your materials differently.

Look at how bookstores merchandize their materials. Grocery stores locate candy and potato chips near checkout stands to encourage impulse buying. Libraries must merchandize to promote library materials. You could "market" certain materials by locating them near the circulation desk.

Using statistics is the best way to find out whether your library is providing optimum service, and with an automated circulation system they are easier to obtain. Increased statistics can be useful in obtaining more book-buying money, in acquiring additional staff or maintaining a high quality of service, and in considering a change of hours: attendance figures will show when a library is heavily used. Probably the most accurate way to record attendance is with an electronic meter at the exit or entrance, which will automatically count who enters or leaves. A turnstile gate allows only one person to enter at a time while with a swing gate a group may enter with only one person counted. Also an hourly head count could be done, possibly with a hand counter. A change of hours could better use staff and be more useful to patrons. Statistics can also be useful in determining which services have little or no use, which could lead to a decision to discontinue the service or to publicize it more.

Keeping circulation statistics is vital to the library. Some things to count: number of books checked out (categorize books according to type), interlibrary loan activity, numbers of audiovisuals, periodicals, and paperbacks circulated, program attendance, money collected (break money down into fines), charges for photocopy rights, number of registered borrowers.

The presentation of the statistics can vary from software to software program (see Figure 1.13).

Knowing how many of which kinds of materials have circulated is a good way to decide how to spend your collection funds. Careful maintenance of statistics is important because knowing which materials are used helps determine future purchasing and justify budget requests.

Accurate circulation records can help you know which days are the busiest and thus help you determine work schedules and hours of operation. For public libraries these records can be shown to the library board or governing body to prove how the library is used.

Some library department heads may file annual reports giving yearly totals for budgets, circulation, and money spent on books. You may need to contribute statistics to an annual report for your library.

Financial Responsibilities

Budgets are a fundamental part of libraries' control mechanisms. Dollar figures are used as a common means of communicating. Access services generates income from fines, overdues, privileges, and photocopying.

If a bill is not paid what are your options? Suspend privileges? Hire a collection agency? Notify police? Take a loss? Arrest patron for nonpayment? Your library must decide how far it wishes to pursue these collection matters.

Billing

The automated circulation system has made this part of the circulation operation much easier. The system generates all notices and billing statements. The number of staff needed to process billing has decreased because of automation. To

Figure 1.13

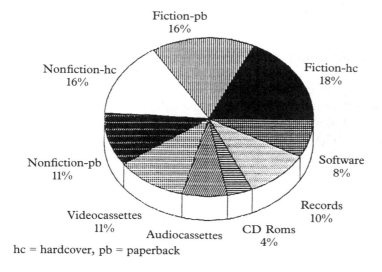

CIRCULATING MATERIALS

Fiction-pb
16%

Nonfiction-hc
16%

Fiction-hc
18%

Software
8%

Records
10%

Nonfiction-pb
11%

Videocassettes
11%

Audiocassettes

CD Roms
4%

hc = hardcover, pb = paperback

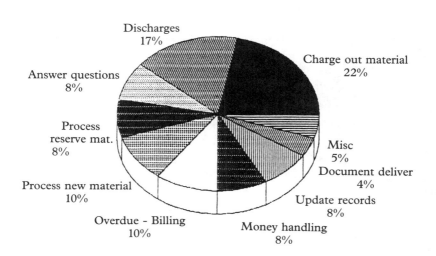

DESK ACTIVITIES

Discharges
17%

Charge out material
22%

Answer questions
8%

Process
reserve mat.
8%

Misc
5%

Document deliver
4%

Process new material
10%

Update records
8%

Overdue - Billing
10%

Money handling
8%

manually bill and send notices is tedious and time consuming work.

Auditing

Your institution has its own money handling procedures. There is no excuse for not knowing the procedures and then following them. Written procedures are necessary for training staff in handling money. Care must be taken when dealing with financial transactions. Remember to follow all policies and procedures. There is an auditing function built into many institutions; the people there can check on the operation at any time.

2
Information Delivery

The Case of the Disappearing Salesperson

During the weekly department heads meeting, the decision is reached to replace the staff photocopier. The staff copier is used by administration, various departments, and interlibrary loan. Marge, because of her knowledge of photocopiers, contacts several companies and arranges demonstrations.

At the beginning of one demonstration the sales representative claims that her photocopier never jams. Ten minutes later the representative is on her knees clearing jams. After all of the demonstrations, a cost analysis of each machine is calculated, references are checked, and then a photocopier is selected. The chosen machine is to be delivered and running within three weeks. Soon the troubles begin. First, the photocopier is delivered two weeks late. It then sits unassembled for another week before service comes. The salesperson neglects to coordinate the installation with service. During this period, the salesperson neither returns Marge's calls nor pays any visits to the library. The salesperson seems to have disappeared.

Unfortunately, this is not an isolated incident. After a sale or when a sale is unlikely, the normally pesky salesperson becomes difficult to reach.

This scenario also reflects differences between a company's sales and service department. The salesperson's first priority is the commission, while the service department's priority is maintenance of the machines. Conflict arises from the incompatibility of their respective goals. When it comes to information delivery, equipment is the key to fast and reliable service. You may have the staff and information ready but if the equipment is not functioning the delivery of your information becomes impossible.

What Is Information Delivery?

This chapter focuses on the dissemination of information. Librarians should never make the mistake of placing the emphasis on the physical object to be delivered. The vehicle changes over time but the information remains. Increasingly, delivery is the part of access services gaining the most interest. In recent years, library literature has become inundated with the impact of automation, electronic revolution, and telefacsimile (FAX) on interlibrary loan.

People and equipment are at the delivery's core, with service as the goal. This belief sometimes is overshadowed by journal articles where the authors would have you believe number crunching is the sole concern of information delivery. First, justification for information delivery should not be as a source of library income. You should be conscious of managing a cost effective operation but fast reliable service must be the first priority.

Patrons

A library cannot possibly contain everything that its patrons want today or will want tomorrow for research, education, or entertainment. Economics, budgetary constraints, length of library existence, space, and timing are all factors preventing this from happening. A library's existence is contingent on fulfilling its patrons' needs. Any library, whatever the size, can meet these needs by obtaining materials from other libraries. The number of volumes a library owns is not important as long as other library collections are accessible.

The goal of information delivery is giving information as

quickly as possible to your own patrons and supplying information to other libraries for requests from their patrons. Children should not be forgotten. Children have information needs and sometimes you must provide resource sharing for them as well. Interlibrary loan is the most well-known delivery process. Some patrons choose to photocopy their own material, thereby bypassing the supervised system. These variations of the delivery process center on getting information as quickly as possible to the patrons.

Let's say you are the interlibrary loan librarian at a medical school library. At 8:30 a.m. you receive an urgent request on your telefacsimile machine. The request comes in marked "*rush*: for patient care." You first verify that your library carries the journal and has received that issue. Once you know that, someone must retrieve the issue from the stacks. Depending on the FAX machine you may or may not have to photocopy the article. Assuming all goes as planned, you transmit the article to the requestor. Unfortunately, that does not complete the process. Finally, you bill the requestor and collect the money. And, do not forget the need for statistics. Now look back at all the steps that must be accomplished before you complete the process.

At the local public library, a patron looks for a book on raising horses. The book is not at her library but a neighboring town's library has that particular book. A firm working on a $3 million proposal needs articles from international business journals subscribed to at the local university library. Professor X, researching medieval musical instruments, needs a book available only from a French university library. Again, not owning the book is relatively unimportant when you nevertheless have access to it. If your library can get it fairly quickly, that is just as good as owning it. Commercial document delivery services such as ERIC allow patrons to bypass libraries completely.

Time is an important consideration. For example, a request may be filled in one hour or take weeks, depending on the network system, resources, equipment, and urgency. Complicating the situation even more, the delivery process is set in an evolving information environment.

The Information Environment

The external environment consists of those elements outside the library that dramatically affect library operations. Examples of this include government funding, the economic state of your community, health care, research, technology, and education. Today, the external environment continuously undergoes rapid changes with far-reaching effects. In this fast-paced world, information is bought, sold, or shared with people who expect that their information needs will be met quickly.

Having access to information throughout the world, people are generally better informed today. Radio and television bring information simultaneously to people around the world. Competition among corporations in a global marketplace is strong. Today, the results of a scientific experiment are published and tomorrow they reach the evening news. Satellite dishes, facsimile, microchips, and telecommunications are now common words in our vocabulary. Computers are fast becoming as common as televisions in homes, schools, and offices. This growing dependence on technology has altered information delivery.

In libraries, computer searching is done by librarians but patrons also have remote access to on-line library catalogs and databases from their homes or offices. End-user computing is becoming more and more common. These electronic systems open up resources to patrons far beyond the library walls.

Today, user friendly products such as modified online databases, compact disc databases, and online databases are available directly to end users. You can check the weather, buy stocks, or use electronic bulletin boards at home by using commercial services, such as Prodigy or Compuserve with a personal computer and modem.

The information explosion has complicated the publishing world, with many more journal titles being published even with the cost of materials increasing rapidly. Compact disc databases open up access to unpublished materials available only from universities. The patrons' information world expands daily.

With all of these changes and new sources of information,

it is not surprising to see information delivery affected. Patrons cannot afford to purchase all of their information needs; so, they must rely on libraries. Still, technology plays only a part in information delivery. Accommodating the information needs of the patron requires commitment beyond the computer. Libraries must fill basic service needs. This is as true now as it was in 1954:

> More attention will be given in public libraries to ease of users. Return receptacles at the curb will become more popular; new libraries will include drive-in windows in their plans and where land is available, off-street parking areas for patrons will be provided. Messenger service to expedite the delivery and return of books to busy people will be used to a greater extent, and service to convalescent and old people's home is likely to be extended. In short, ease of use and extension of service will dominate future trends in circulation systems.*

Libraries have changed in the past four decades but the same quest for easier access still continues. Making information accessible to the patron is the overriding concern.

Information Delivery

Interlibrary Loan

Sometimes, patrons need access to information that is not available locally. Interlibrary loan is the oldest type of cooperative or resource sharing structure. Requesting materials for the patron and supplying materials to other libraries that have made requests for their patrons is the function of interlibrary loan. Since libraries cannot house everything its patrons want, sometimes you request and other times you supply materials. This resource sharing necessary among libraries requires the interlibrary loan operation. Libraries must cooperate with each other to survive the economic constraints of growing numbers of materials available and escalating prices.

*Bousfield, Humphrey G., p. 175.

Every library handles their interlibrary loan process differently. A separate section with its own staff or a staff of one or twenty may perform the duties. With such diversity in staff sizes, increased costs, and demand for information, increased reliance on networking has resulted. The actual requesting is accomplished in many ways.

The OCLC system includes an interlibrary loan feature which permits a borrowing library to enter a request for an item and to designate lenders. The system will bump the request after a specific period of time to the next library.

The National Library of Medicine began implementation of a similar program, DOCLINE, an automated interlibrary loan request routing and referral system. The system includes the use of online linkages to bibliographic, institutional, and serials holding information and the use of automated routing, as well as a strong resource sharing network.

Users of DOCLINE receive monthly reports of the number of requests filled and not filled as a borrower and as a lender, and annual lists of requested serial titles. By October 1988 there were over 1600 libraries using DOCLINE with nearly 1.3 million requests routed at an overall fill rate of 92 percent. The DOCLINE system uses the preexisting Regional Library Network.*

High volume information delivery service will remove a large number of items from the shelves as well as increase reshelving work. In-house users may be inconvenienced and may compete for materials and photocopy facilities. A closed-stack library that does not circulate materials can provide the most efficient delivery service. Information delivery puts pressure on stack maintenance. Materials need to be on the shelf for your patrons and to fulfill interlibrary loan requests quickly.

Requests and materials are sent and received via mail, UPS, phone, electronic mail, and facsimile machine. The facsimile machine has reduced delivery time from days to minutes.

---

*Dutcher, Gale A. "DOCLINE: A National Automated Interlibrary Loan Request Routing and Referral System." Information Technology and Libraries 8, 4 (1989): 359.

Figure 2.1

```
                        Library
                   FAX COVER SHEET

Date:  ____/_____/_____
To:    _____   Fax #  _____
       _____

From:  Library
       Street
       City, St.
       Fax #:
       Phone #:

Page 1 of _____

Message:


If there is any problem with this fax transaction please notify
(000) 000-0000.
```

Facsimile (FAX) Machine

Today, the facsimile machine has become commonplace in libraries. With a FAX you can instantaneously send copies of articles to other libraries equipped with compatible machines, or communicate quickly with libraries and other agencies.

The supplying library staff enters the phone number of the requesting library. After the phone connection is made, a scanner reads the cover letter (see Figure 2.1) and document.

Many FAX machines feature two or three scanning resolution settings. It may include settings for photograph only, photograph with text, and text settings. A higher resolution scan contains more data and will take longer to transmit.

Facsimile works by distinguishing between the dark and light areas on the page. This is translated into electrical bits that are sent over phone lines. The receiving unit recreates the grid of light and dark that form shapes we call letters.

Several state-of-the-art machines include a copier style platen which allows copying directly from bound materials to be sent immediately or into memory to be sent later without any paper copy. These machines also have laser printers, which print with plain paper. Many units print with thermal paper. Paper

The FAX machine.

costs differ from manufacturer to manufacturer and sometimes users are warned that maintenance problems may occur if the wrong paper is used; therefore a library could be locked into buying from one paper supplier.

Problems occur with copy quality if phone lines are noisy. Newer machines can fine tune out the noise and if necessary redial busy phone numbers.

Some questions to consider: How will a FAX capability fit into the library and interlibrary loan work flow and procedures? Are patrons using commercial document delivery services instead of the library? In this time of "I want it now," are patrons as willing to wait for materials? Are patron expectations too high? Will every request come in marked *rush?* Once your FAX phone number is published, be prepared for an onslaught of requests.

The convenience of the facsimile machine raises several issues. First is the possibility of copyright violation when the requestor, in addition to the FAXed article, requests a photocopy be sent; therefore they will have two copies of the same article. Also, the time element for processing and mailing costs place extra burdens on the supplying library.

Libraries must learn to trust the facsimile quality. It seems a real waste of time and money to perform both procedures. Libraries should upgrade their equipment if the quality of the FAXed article is that poor.

Some practical issues such as ordering of supplies—thermal roll paper, photocopy paper, laser bond paper, toner, cleaning kit, and developer—must be addressed and included in the cost of the operation.

Labor costs are difficult to calculate because the work is integrated into the regular interlibrary loan operations. Lower labor costs come with features such as automatic document feeder, automatic receive and send, speed dialing, and automatic redialing features. As trust in the technology increases, labor costs will decrease. Eventually, staff will start the process and then only return for the confirmation. Training is important in reducing labor costs.

Facsimile communication charges depend on distance, time of transmission, and speed. You may decide to store the document in memory and then transmit it during off-peak times. Whenever you transmit a document it does take longer than a telephone call. Your telephone charges will be higher.

Linking FAXes with personal computers by means of facsimile boards and software is now being promoted.*

Will the FAX machine revolutionize document delivery? Is it just an intermediate step? What will replace it?

Other Uses for a FAX

Between branches of a library system, the FAX machine can be used to transmit articles or table of contents, and communicate

---

*Walton, Robert. *"Are PC Fax Boards Good for Libraries."* Library Journal 115, 5 (1990): 66–68.

messages. For example, Library Y no longer subscribes to a journal but Library X will fax the table of contents to the library. Now patrons at Library Y can determine if they need one of the articles. Facsimile messages eliminate phone tag. Patrons may also renew materials using the facsimile technology.

Ultimately, need, cost, speed, and user satisfaction are the factors that a library must consider when determining whether or not to use facsimile.

Verification

Should interlibrary loan requests be verified? Verification is the corroboration of citation information through indexes, catalogs, and bibliographies, all of which may exist either on the computer or in print. Bibliographic verification for interlibrary loan is required by the American Library Association Interlibrary Loan Code. The verification process is very time consuming. Patrons fill out requests sloppily and incompletely. Libraries accepting the requests must screen patron requests. By the time the request arrives it must be filled out properly and accurately. There are some librarians who feel the verification step is unnecessary.* The issue is still under discussion.

Mailing

Materials are still sent through the mail, UPS, or other methods. The normal procedures and policies of circulation may need modification. What about renewals, holds, recalls? Will a longer loan period be necessary to allow for transit time. Are you sending a film that needs to be somewhere on a certain day?

The materials must be packaged for shipping short or long distances. Air bubble packing material can best protect the

---

*Bell, Jo Ann, and Speer, Susan. "Bibliographic Verification." College and Research Libraries 49, 6 (1988): 500.

materials. How will you send the materials? Will fragile materials be loaned?

Personnel time is the largest cost factor of interlibrary loan. Direct costs include the cost of equipment, supplies, photocopying, postage or delivery service, telephone or telecommunication charges. Indirect costs include the cost of circulation tasks (hold, recall, renew, charge, discharge), reshelving, statistical reporting, and wear and tear on the collection.

Bookmobiles

It is estimated that there currently are 1000 bookmobile operations around the country, and during the period 1979–1984, the typical library saw a 2 percent increase in the number of rural people served by the bookmobile.*

Bookmobiles offer a unique service, especially to rural patrons. The patron who travels to the library to borrow materials is usually not a customer of bookmobiles.

Farms are isolated from libraries and farm work hours limit access to libraries. Under such situations, bookmobiles offer a solution. Bookmobiles are also an effective means of reaching across the physical and communication barriers that are inherent in the lives of migrant farm workers. In these settings, flexibility in circulation policies is imperative. The materials may range from paperback books to audiotapes.

Services and materials vary from community to community. Print and nonprint resources, children's programs, reference services, and interlibrary loan are all possible from a bookmobile operation.

The computer age has not bypassed the bookmobile. One out of ten mobiles has a microcomputer on board for circulation, with CLSI tending to be the favorite system.† You may decide to

---

*Vavrek, Bernard. "Rural Warriors." Library Journal 115, 4 (1990): 56.

†Vavrek, Bernard, p. 57.

circulate only paperback materials because of a high loss of materials. Every bookmobile route has its own concerns.

A growing segment of the population is the older adult. Older adults may not be able to drive or walk to a library. Taxis are expensive and may be difficult to hail. Public transportation may not exist or be difficult to use physically and mentally for the older adult. If library delivery services are not available, some older adults are cut off from library use. Active, healthy older adults should be encouraged to volunteer in the library. They could help transport or deliver materials to retirement complexes, hospitals, and senior centers.

Homebound, hospitalized, or incarcerated people are other target groups for delivery services. If your library cannot afford a bookmobile operation, books by mail service could fill the delivery need. The options are limited only by your imagination.

Some concerns to consider for bookmobile services are lack of staff, financial support, and the inability to carry enough materials. Mechanical upkeep is the most significant challenge and transportation costs will be the biggest expense. Inclement weather may also render the service inoperable.

Bookmobile operations and any delivery service require study and a commitment from the library. Whatever is chosen, all possible resources must be committed to the operation.

Campus Delivery

A recent trend in academic libraries has been the establishment of information delivery programs in which staff collect and deliver materials to patrons on campus. This service may initially bring up more questions than answers.

Who are your eligible users?

Faculty, staff, graduates, and undergraduates? Local individuals or businesses not affiliated with your campus, perhaps for a fee or for good public relations?

What kind of requests?

Requests will most likely be for in-house materials. Do you

do subject-based (i.e., not author-title) requests? Will you handle requests for both entertainment-related and research materials? How many requests per individual will you accept at one time? Should you set a limit? (If a certain turnaround time is guaranteed, you must limit the number of requests.) Will you supply photocopies or actual materials? Issues of loan period, copyright, and circulation policy must be addressed. Can you obtain signed statements for permission to use ID numbers? Is any type of material to be off limits, such as noncirculating items?

How will requests be submitted?

Requests may come in via letter, telephone, electronic mail, or FAX. You may consider designing your own form (see Figure 2.2). Telephone submission is convenient for patrons but increases the chance of error. With an answering machine you have also a greater chance of incomplete data. In either case you will not know about problems until later.

How will requests be delivered?

How will you handle retrieval and delivery of items? Will responsibility for delivery of materials be in the hands of library staff or the campus mail service? Do you deliver to one library or to its branches, travel library to library, or offer direct delivery to the patron's door?

What if material is not on the shelf?

Do you provide other circulation services such as recall, interlibrary loan, holds, or search? When do you let patron know material is unavailable? How much staff is needed?

What about funding?

Will you charge user fees? Additional fees for extras such as referrals, rushes? Will you accept cash, check, charge cards, or department accounts? How do you market the service?

Knowledge of the availability of the material in the public catalog is as important as knowing what the library owns. Full document delivery to campus users should be instituted as soon as remote access to local files or an online catalog becomes available.

Figure 2.2

```
                    Photocopying Request
Please complete a separate form for each item requested.
PLEASE PRINT.
PERIODICAL                          BOOK CALL NO.
Periodical _____   Author    _____
_____    Title     _____
Volume _____ Issue _____ Date ____         _____
Author _____  Edition _____ Place
Title of Article _____  Publisher _____Year _
_____    Series   _____
Inclusive Pagination _____  Inclusive paging  _____
_____
_____


Name: _____  PAYMENT
Address: _____   Cash
_____     Charge account
Status and Dept. _____
Telephone _____   DELIVERY
                                      Hold
                                      Send by
Why request not filled:
```

There are many policies and procedures that go into running any effective delivery service. Issues will keep surfacing.

Electronic Mail

Electronic mail (e-mail) systems allow creation and transmission of messages. The receiver can read the messages, answer them, store them electronically, forward them to another individual, print a copy of them, or erase them. The best benefit of e-mail is the elimination of phone tag and the frustration of not reaching someone. E-mail can be used for interlibrary loan or document requests. You can broadcast questions and ask for resolutions. This is one way to discover possible solutions and problems through a network.

Commercial Vendors

With the new competitive information marketplace, libraries compete with commercial information brokers for document delivery services. Chemical Abstracts Service, ERIC, and University Microfilms International are serious competitors. Quite often companies are adding, changing, and deleting delivery options. The "1-900" telephone-number companies could become another source for ordering information and documents.

Companies now market many databases in compact disc format. The technology allows the ability to merge sound, graphics and videodisc peripherals, and electronic full texts. It is very appealing. Full text searching on compact disc encourages more browsing with no threat of high connect time costs. Because patrons spend more time searching, the library may end up with more requests. Establishing procedures ahead of time will save staff and patrons hours of frustration.

Businesses, such as law firms or pharmaceutical companies, may purchase privileges and hire people to copy articles. To bypass purchasing library privileges, companies may employ library staff to copy materials after work hours.

Photocopiers

Photocopiers are a valuable library tool for information delivery. Before photocopiers, patrons had less access to information. Photocopying revolutionized libraries. Patrons no longer had to travel to read materials that their library did not own. Patrons could copy an article and read it at home. Access to information became easier and quicker. Libraries have a built-in clientele for photocopying. The goals of the library in providing on-site photocopying are service and reduction of theft and mutilation. The quality of service is highly dependent on the equipment. Concerns include equipment performance, money handling, copyright issues, staffing, profitability, and vandalism. The availability of responsive maintenance and repair

Photocopier.

service is the most important factor when making any equipment decisions.

The library's number one goal is service, not profit. Do not expect the revenue generated by photocopy operation to cover all or most of the costs associated with the service. Often photocopy staffing costs must be subsidized to some degree from another part of the library budget.

Operations

Self-service photocopying operations have variations: coin-operated machines that may or may not give change, and copy cards or mechanical or electronic auditrons. Any system requiring coins makes it necessary for the library to have a supply of

Card reader unit.

small change available. A wall mounted dispenser of copy cards for purchases on re-encoding comes in handy evenings and weekends.

A card reader unit connected to a photocopier accepts a debit card with number of copies or a dollar amount. When patrons purchase cards you may accept cash or credit card, or charge back to institutional fund accounts.

At some libraries, management of self-service photocopiers has been contracted out to a vendor. Under this arrangement, the library receives a share of the revenue. At other libraries, another department outside the library has responsibility for the copy service.

If you contract out the operation, you must have everything in writing to protect your library. The contract is a legal document specifying hardware and services provided by the vendor.

For example, in the contract you specify that the equipment must have the following:

1. a coin-op, card reader device which accepts and gives change;
2. a paper supply of at least 500, 8½"×11" sheets;
3. the capability to make copies "lighter" or "darker";
4. service personnel who can respond to repair calls within 4 hours;
5. a flat, stationary document glass, with a beveled or dropped edge to accommodate tight bindings; and
6. generated copies that are clear, clean and sharp and that can include photographs.

In addition you the librarian must:

7. maintain a relationship with the service-providers and insure that all machines are kept in good working order; and
8. keep a cash refund account at designated places to refund money lost in the machines.

While the library, in theory, may be relieved of demands on its own staff when a vendor manages the photocopy service, in reality the library staff often must deal with complaints, and must often fill machines with paper, and clear paper jams.

An option to contracting out the photocopy service is for library staff to run a self-service operation. The library budget and revenues from the operation fund the machines, supplies, and labor.

The library orders and pays for paper, copy cards, and supplies. Staff service the machines by clearing jams, adding dry ink, and paper, and performing minor repairs.

Mediated copy services are those in which staff does the copying. The patron is usually asked to bring the materials to be copied to a specific location or the library may provide the additional service of paging the material that is to be copied.

Prices for this service vary, but usually are higher than for self-service copying because of the staff time involved.

Selection

The photocopier chosen can be a leverage point with the sales company. People come into the library, use the copier and form opinions of that machine. This affects any future purchasing decision by the patron. If the patron is looking for an office photocopier, their opinion of that machine may color their perception. "At the library it was never working," may be the thought. This is a bargaining chip for the library. You are promoting their company's name. The company has an added incentive in keeping the machines running.

Investigate the state of the art of such equipment thoroughly. Be aware of what is happening, attend conferences where vendors display their latest equipment, and check with other libraries.

Cost

You should perform cost comparisons of photocopy delivery methods. But in addition to cost, you need to consider patron satisfaction. Running a photocopying service has public relations value and good will potential which may overshadow cost.

Photocopy costs=personnel (salary, wages, benefits)+equipment+maintenance+supplies is one simple formula. Will you purchase, rent, or lease equipment? You should do a cost comparison based on your library. (See Figure 2.3.)

Service

Is company service available? What is its response time? Investigate service maintenance contracts. Exactly what do they include and how much do they cost? If maintenance is performed by library staff, then training, written instructions, tools, and machine parts need to be on hand.

Can staff do minor servicing or must a company representative always do all repairs? What is the turnaround time for

Figure 2.3

Comparative Advantages of Lease and Purchase Arrangements

Factor	Lease	Purchase overtime	Purchase outright
Capital Requirements			
Maintenance Cost			
Supply Cost			
Ownership			
Tax Advantage			
Upgrade/trade-in			
Resell			
Cost per Copy			
Length of Agreement			

service? Will the machine be out of order for long periods of time?

Photocopiers must be used in a way that guarantees safe working conditions for staff and patrons. Under normal operations, when the machines are located in a ventilated area and are regularly serviced, any potential hazards will be reduced. Staff need to be fully trained in disposing of dry ink, clearing paper jams without being burned, and cleaning the machines. Used dry ink or toner should be placed in sealed bags and arranged carefully for disposal. Remember to recycle paper.

Ozone! Photocopiers have been identified as a source of ozone. The only solution is a well ventilated, air-conditioned room with air vented to the outside.

Complaints

Little is more frustrating than repeatedly seeing a piece of equipment in need of repair, with an out of order sign, and having to wait days for service. The performance level of such equipment as computers and photocopiers can make or break a work day and cause you to go home happy or miserable.

You will hear complaints about the photocopy equipment and have many headaches. Personally, I have worked with an outside vendor who maintained machines and card readers, with library staff (students) filling machines with paper. Also I have worked with library-run operations. I have used other libraries' operations. There does not seem to be such a thing as the perfect photocopying operation. It is extremely difficult to manage; the same problems surface over and over again: "I have been waiting" "Where is it?" "Not enough machines—need more machines." "The machine ate my money [or copy card]." "It erased my card." "The quality is poor." "Machine just jammed." "Need more paper."

One thing to remember is why you have photocopiers: to provide good, reasonably priced copies as a substitute for loaning materials so as to make materials in general more readily available to all patrons. Let patrons know that service has been called (see Figures 2.4 and 2.5).

Preservation issues, such as handling of materials when photocopying, must be addressed in staff training and with patrons when possible.

Unfortunately, photocopiers are a source of frustration for you and the staff. You will spend more time on the operation than you ever thought possible. You must be prepared for annoyance.

Financial Aspects

Photocopy operations with coin operated machines require money to be collected, counted, and deposited. Usually, a

Figure 2.4

OUT OF ORDER

DATE / INITIALS

Figure 2.5

PHOTOCOPY PROBLEM REPORT

Name _____ Date ___/___/___ Time _____ am   pm

Machine Serial Number _____

Problem _____
_____
_____

Error code _____

Action taken _____
_____
_____

Card reader box number _____

Problem _____
_____
_____

Action taken _____
_____

change machine should be available also. Somewhere there may be a cash register for copy card sales, photocopying done by staff, and other purchases. Information delivery takes in money. Your library will have its own money handling procedures. Money handling is time consuming and takes a lot of thought and effort. There is no one way to deal with the money issue. Security is always of concern when money is present.

Copyright

Copyright touches ILL, audiovisual, unsupervised photo-copying, supervised photocopying, reserve collection, and software. What is copyright?

Copyright is protection for the authors against unauthorized copying of their works. Copyright keeps with authors the right to copy the work, the right to prepare derivative works, the right to distribute copies of the work and the right to perform the work publicly. Copyright protection begins as soon as the work is created and is in effect until 50 years after the author's death; or, in the case of a work with multiple authors, 50 years after creation.

Copyright protects the *expression* of ideas. The idea or thought itself is not copyrightable—only the tangible expression of the idea is protected by law. Copyright covers books, articles, music, paintings, photographs, plays, computer programs, and practically anything else.

Works created by United States government employees in the course of their employment are in the public domain. Some items such as public domain software programs and written works that are intended to be copied will clearly state that they may be freely copied. There are companies that sell disks of public domain software.

The publisher's copyright covers a journal as a collective whole.

Copyright law permits libraries to make photocopies upon the request of a patron provided that the copies become property of the user and are within the "fair use" guidelines.

Fair use generally applies to the making of single copies for personal use. Since permission to reproduce multiple copies of copyrighted materials must be obtained from the copyright owner, library photocopy services will usually only make single copies of copyrighted materials. Many libraries have established guidelines to aid in complying with the criteria.

A library may, on a patron's behalf, obtain through interlibrary loan service an article from a journal that it does not subscribe to. The making of a single copy of one article from a journal or small part of a book for private study, scholarship, or research is "fair use." Copyright law requires that the copy becomes the property of the patron lest an accumulation of interlibrary loan copies substitutes for the purchase of a subscription by the borrowing library.

Guidelines accompanying the law allow the library to request, within any calendar year, no more than five articles published in the last five years of any one journal. For copyrighted works other than journals, a requesting library may receive up to five portions of any given work. These ILL limitations do not apply if the requesting library has in force, or has entered, a subscription to the periodical; if the requesting library owns the title or other copyrighted work that it has nevertheless requested because the materials were not reasonably available; or if the periodical(s) were published more than five years prior to the date the request was made. After that, the request would be notice that demand is high enough at the library to consider purchasing a subscription to the journal. Here is where a system like DOCLINE is important. At year end a list of journals and number of times requested is produced.

Placing multiple photocopies of journal articles on reserve may present copyright problems. Libraries usually accept a faculty member's photocopy of an article and place it on reserve. Also libraries will make one copy of an article from a journal and place it on reserve.

Here is the warning:

Notice Warning Concerning Copyright Restrictions

The copyright law of the United States (Title 17, United States Code) governs the making of photocopies or other reproductions of copyrighted material. Under certain conditions specified in the law, libraries and archives may furnish a photocopy or other reproduction. One of these specified conditions is that the photocopy or reproduction is not to be "used for any purpose other than private study, scholarship, or research." If a user makes a request for, or later uses, a photocopy or reproduction for purposes in excess of "fair use," that user may be liable for copyright infringement. This institution reserves the right to refuse to accept a copying order if, in its judgment, fulfillment of the order would involve violations of the copyright law.

A library may list its own guidelines:

1. One copy of an article or chapter;
2. No more than 50 pages of an article or chapter;
3. Only one article per issue or one chapter per book;
4. No more than three articles per volume.

You should should put up copyright warning and guideline signs in the photocopy area, interlibrary loan desk, circulation desk, and any other locations to protect yourself. Issues of circulating software and copyright violations have become common topics.

But on May 1, 1990, the Senate passed S. 198, a bill to prohibit the commercial rental, lease, or lending of computer software. The bill would exempt nonprofit libraries and nonprofit educational institutions from its provisions. Nonprofit libraries lending software must affix to each software package the following notice:

> Warning: This computer program is protected under the copyright law. Making a copy of this program without permission of the copyright owner is prohibited. Anyone copying this program without permission of the copyright owner may be subject to payment of up to $100,000 damages and in some cases, imprisonment for up to one year.

The Register of Copyrights at the Library of Congress, must review the library exemption in three years, and after consulting with copyright owners and librarians, report to Congress. In other provisions, the transfer of possession of a lawfully made copy of computer software by a nonprofit educational institution among faculty, staff, students, or to another school is not prohibited. The bill does not apply to computer game cartridges.*

*Henderson, Carol C. "Washington Hotline." College & Research Libraries 51, 6 (1990): 523.

The videotape copyright issue is shrouded in shades of gray. Librarians should adhere as closely as possible to the letter of the law but continue to abide by any of American Library Association's recommended guidelines.*

The Future

Information delivery and increasing cost of materials will continue. Resource sharing and cooperation will become even more important. Future technology will be applied to information delivery as equipment becomes more affordable. The information explosion will continue; people will continue to research and write. Information delivery bridges technical services (materials need to be ordered, processed, and claimed) and reference (someone must tell people how). Access services gets the information to the patron. Will libraries continue to loan original materials or loan only facsimiles?

Focusing on information, not the object, will be the key to dealing with upcoming changes. The physical format is only the vehicle.

*Here are a few sources on the topic: Charles Vlcek, Copyright Policy Development: A Resource Book for Educators *(Friday Harbor, Wash.: Copyright Information Services, 1987); Ivan R. Bender and Hazelmeier,* Copyright: What Every School, College and Public Library Should Know *(Deerfield, Ill.: Association for Informational Media and Equipment, 1987); Jerome K. Miller,* Video/Copyright Seminar *(Friday Harbor, Wash.: Copyright Information Services, 1987), audiocassette; Virginia Helm,* What Educators Should Know About Copyright *(Bloomington, Ind.: Phi Delta Kappa Educational Foundation, 1986).*

3
Patrons and Security

Curse on Book Thieves

Found on the door of an ancient monastic library in Barcelona, Spain:

> For him that stealeth a book
> From this library
> Let it change into a serpent
> In his hand and rend him.
> Let him be struck with palsy
> And all his members be blasted.
> Let him languish in pain,
> Crying aloud for mercy and
> Let there be no surcease to his
> Agony 'till he sink in dissolution.
> Let bookworms gnaw his entails
> In token of the worm that dieth not,
> And when at last he goeth to
> His final judgment,
> Let flames of hell consume him
> Forever and aye.

The Fur Coat and the Razor Blade

While Marge is on the phone a commotion erupts at the circulation desk. She excuses herself and quickly goes to investigate. There at the circulation desk is a female patron, who keeps setting off the security system but apparently has no books. Finally, Marge notices the lining of the woman's fur coat bulging. Marge asks the woman to take off her coat. In the coat's lining are two library books that have not been charged out. Security is called and the patron is taken away by a guard.

This episode reminds Marge of the razor blade method. A patron was caught with stolen pages from journals. Luckily, one of the pages happened to have a security tag on it. The patron confessed to the theft and admitted using a razor blade, hidden under a Bandaid, to cut out pages. After both these events, Marge finds herself suspicious of anyone wearing a fur coat or a Bandaid on a finger.

Unfortunately, throughout time there has been the need to protect library materials and equipment from theft and mutilation. Security is dependent upon a variety of factors that correspond with each organization or library's perception of its mission and goals. In addition, security and ease of access are tied to space and staffing.

This chapter focuses on patrons, security measures, the confidentiality of circulation records, and social issues such as the homeless and latchkey children.

The Patron

Sometimes patrons behave in a manner that is irritating, inappropriate, or upsetting to other patrons and staff. It is difficult dealing with a disturbed patron. A run-in with a patron can be scary, annoying, or time consuming. Such experiences can make the job miserable.

The following descriptions are of patron behaviors that staff may encounter:

1. *Angry verbal abuse*—an extremely abusive and threatening argument about a fine, checking books out without appropriate library card, special privileges, a search. Doctor Angst has been known to cause new staff to quiver with each demand.

2. *Arrogant*—"I am better than you"; has the "help me first" syndrome.
3. *Destruction of library materials*—vandalism, mutilation, theft.

   Mary Alice does not want to wait for a photocopier, so she rips out the article and leaves the library.
4. *Personal hygiene problems*—odors; may also be a staff problem.

   Joe Charles, a foreign student, works as a shelver in an academic library. In his country, he is almost a king but at the library whenever he leaves an area, his odor remains.
5. *Refusal to abide by library rules*—eating and drinking.
6. *Bizarre but nonthreatening.*

   Louise Patron passes the time aimlessly moving through the stacks.
7. *Disruptive behavior.*

   Once a week, a patron or two complain of singing in the stacks but no one has ever gotten a description of the offender.
8. *Suspicious lurking.*
9. *Obscene phone calls.*

   Every night at 9:30 p.m. the phone rings, and the caller says nothing but heavy breathing.
10. *Sexual harassment.*

    One young professional man more than flirts with the young women of the staff.
11. *Chronic complainer*—what do you believe, when is an excuse the truth.

    Marlene the complainer: Whenever she walks in, the staff hide. At least once a week she complains about the heat, lost books, hours, and the state of the union.
12. *Irate parents*—why did you let my child see that video, read that book?

    John and Mary Parent storm in and confront the circulation desk staff about allowing John, Jr., age 12, to charge out a PG-13 video.

13. *Teenagers* (gangs, graffiti).
14. *Chatty patrons*—sometimes you have someone who just is lonely and wants to talk.

Mr. Plant comes in every couple of days to talk with whomever happens to be at the circulation desk.

15. *Disruptive children*—playing tag.

Of course if staff feels in any way threatened, they should get help immediately. Hanging up on obscene callers should be a rule of thumb.

It is important to establish a routine for handling threats, obscene phone calls, or any emergency. Procedures should be worked out with legal advice and in conjunction with the police.

Here are some hints for dealing with the less dangerous situations:

1. Remain calm, and listen. Handle problems in private, if possible, to avoid any embarrassment. Do not create a scene; it does not project a good image to other patrons. Also, if patrons are explaining why materials were lost, it is better to discuss this in private so that if you waive any fee it will remain an exception.

2. Repeat your request if necessary. Paraphrase the patron's statements to convince them that you are listening. If the person does not understand you, do not raise your voice. Merely rephrase your answer and speak slowly and distinctly.

3. Do not argue with outrageous statements; if they believe what they say, you will not change their minds.

4. Stay in control of the situation; never allow the patron to manipulate you. Be concerned with positively communicating the rationale for policies in order to gain the understanding and cooperation of staff and patrons. When policy is in writing, a patron can see that a refusal is not personal. Keep accurate written records; proof in writing is very useful in justifying actions. If necessary, quietly but firmly and politely tell the patron to quiet down or leave.

5. Avoid humor or personal remarks. Think about a situation where the tables were turned: How would or did you react to a joke made about something you felt strongly about?

6. Get help if needed: alert other staff members, or security. Know when to refer a problem. Staff must not feel that they have to handle it alone. Make certain that a supervisor is told of any incident. Record exactly what happened. You may have a form or choose to develop one (see Figures 3.1 and 3.2). With the security violation form you can record the incidence of individuals who are caught with uncharged materials. You may be able to detect a pattern of abuse.

7. If other staff members need help, support them.

8. Personal verbal or physical abuse should never be tolerated.

9. Non–English-speaking patrons are usually not hard of hearing; do not shout to be understood. You just need to listen, speak slowly and distinctly.

10. Warn others; raise the awareness of staff about offenders and any incident. Include reports of incidents in staff meetings.

11. Do not let it ruin your day. Easier said than done, I know. You must prepare frontline staff to handle this part of the job.

Problems with patrons cannot be ignored because they will never disappear. Training prepares staff to handle these situations.

At any time staff could face a troubling incident. Role playing is one method for staff to act out their worst nightmares. Let staff trade off playing patron and staff roles. Sharing an incident during meetings can be beneficial and therapeutic for the entire staff. Real life is impossible to duplicate, but by practicing scenarios novices can learn from experienced staff the best way to handle situations.

Figure 3.1

COLLECTION SECURITY VIOLATION REPORT

Please print all information, fill out completely and forward
immediately to the attention of your supervisor.

I.   Identification

Name _____   Library _____

Address _____   Date _____

_____ Time _____ AM _____ PM

Phone_(_____)_____

II. Verification

Patron ID # _____

Driver's License (STATE) _____   (NUMBER) _____

Other ID (DESCRIBE)   _____

Status   _____

III. Description of Incident

Check one or more of the following:

Visible in hand _____   In patron's bag ____

Clothing _____

If none of the above, please explain:

_____

Has material been damaged, please explain: _____

Call number or title   _____

Patron's explanation:

IV. Monitor

Please note your impression below:

Inadvertent:

Deliberate:

Other, please explain

Reported by:

Figure 3.2

Accident Report

I.   Identification

    Name

    Address

    Phone

II. Description of Incident

Disabled Patrons

Libraries need to make services, collections, and materials usable and accessible for the disabled, aged, and young patrons by improving access to the library and within the library. The library will need to modify the physical setting, services, and the materials. On July 26, 1990, the President of the United States signed the Americans with Disabilities Act. One way to make sure of the success of any change is to include the patron in the decision making process. It is impossible to see a library as a disabled patron would see it, unless you are disabled. But you should nevertheless try, as open-mindedly as possible.

Take a walk around the outside of the library. Better yet, take along someone who uses a wheelchair to test out the library. How accessible is the library? What about parking lots, walkways, ramps, entrances and exits? Once inside the library examine doors and doorways, stairs and steps, floors, restrooms, elevators, and controls. How high are the stacks, tables, or doorknobs? Are there plenty of signs? Signs for children may need to be different from adult signs. Are there any hazards?

Besides the physical environment, services may need modification. Services such as photocopying, paging, proxy cards, and special equipment may need to be provided. Special equipment such as adjustable height tables, TTY machines, or Kurtzweil reading machines may make it possible for the disabled to access collections without extensive staff assistance. Physical barriers are in many ways easier to overcome than attitudinal barriers.

Attitudes are more difficult to change. A machine alone cannot do this, but when people see the disabled functioning in a library then some of those mental barriers may break down.

Older Adults

Another growing group requiring library services is the older adult. Libraries must reevaluate their services to older adults. Topeka Public Library has a new commitment to target services for the older adult. Their Low Vision Center contains large print books and magazines, magnifiers and reading aids, radio reader service, talking books and a kit with special aids.*

Issues of access, services, and materials for the older adult must be addressed by libraries and their surrounding communities. Older adults should expect trained staff, services, materials, and the physical space to meet their information needs.

Security Issues

Theft and Mutilation of Materials

Theft and mutilation of materials are chronic problems common to all libraries. Over time, lost materials add up to a substantial amount of money. Not only are the materials lost but it may also take money and time to search, order, process, and catalog a replacement, if one can be found.

Is there too much concern over the security of nonprint materials? Videotapes are no longer expensive and back up copies of software are what usually circulate. Unfortunately, any loss results in patron and staff frustration and less confidence in the format.

Although a patron may possess an uncharged item, that does not always mean that a theft is occurring. It is possible the patron forgot he or she had the item. Especially after photocopying, patrons may collect library materials with the rest of their stuff and attempt to leave. So one should always consider that occasionally patrons do merely forget to charge materials out; nevertheless, the majority of thefts are by patrons who deliberately take materials from libraries without charging the materials out.

*Tevis, Jean Ann, and Crawley, Brenda. "Reaching Out to Older Adults." Library Journal 113, 8 (1988): 39.

Patrons may take materials to add to their personal collections but by far the largest number of thefts are by patrons who want to use the materials without the need to return them. Sometimes users take noncirculating materials to use at home. These patrons may or may not return them to the library. Every once in a while you hear of a book reappearing after many years, usually with an apologetic note. And, haven't we all seen library books at used bookstores?

Sometimes patrons conceal materials from other patrons by deliberately misshelving them in an unlikely spot in the stacks. Unfortunately, there is no way to prevent this. Staff may happen to discover a stash.

Mutilation of materials is often done quietly and not discovered until long after the damage has been done. A patron may show up in a panic with a mutilated volume explaining how she needs that missing article immediately. Typically, interlibrary loan must order the article and staff must then tip in the replacement pages. This process takes time and frustrates everyone. The removal of journal articles seems to occur more often in academic libraries.

Another form of mutilation is the cutting out of theft detection tags, thereby allowing the material to leave the library freely. Also, patrons cut out pages, plates, pictures, maps, tables, and diagrams. They also write comments on page margins, make grease and water marks, and "dog-ear" pages.

If patrons perceive that your library has difficult access, short loan periods, limited or nonexistent renewals, or many noncirculating items, you may experience security problems. Also, if keys are not controlled, property is unmarked, or there are few photocopiers which work, security will inevitably be a predicament. Photocopiers especially seem to limit the incidence of theft and mutilation. Finally, if staff does not follow proper procedures, if no systematic renewal of privileges or cards exists, or if exits are guarded carelessly, difficulties will continue.

School libraries have evolved into media centers. Their audiovisual equipment, computers and materials have become more attractive targets for theft. This move from only books to equipment requires a reevaluation of security issues. Locking equipment to tables or shutting drapes and blinds so that people cannot see computer equipment become necessary security steps.

Special security issues arise when dealing with rare materials. For example, rare materials in open stacks may go unprotected and unidentified. Periodically, a reevaluation of materials in the stacks is necessary. Here are some steps to take with known rare books and manuscripts:

1. Offer to photocopy material instead of allowing access to the original.
2. Thoroughly check the identification of any unknown patron.
3. Permit no browsing of materials.
4. Do not allow coats or bags into a secured area.
5. Record and detail all parts to the materials.
6. Allow access to only one item at a time.
7. Whenever possible, use security staff.

The following guidelines developed by the ACRL Rare Books and Manuscripts Sections Security Committee suggest what to do before a theft occurs: appoint a security officer, form a security planning group, publicize rules, establish contact with law enforcement agencies, lobby for legislation, and contact secondhand dealers and work with them to be on guard.

Also, begin a process of reviewing materials in the general collection and open stacks to consider whether materials should be transferred to special collections or a limited access area. After a theft occurs, notify security, evaluate exactly what happened, and notify the library staff and public.*

People

In addition to materials and equipment, you should be alert to personal security issues also. The following is a possible outline for a security training program:

Moffett, William A. "Guidelines Regarding Thefts in Libraries RBMS Security Committee." College and Research Libraries News 49, 3 (1988): 159–162.

I. Establish security objectives
    A. Conduct orientation training for and teach security measures to staff members library wide
    B. Encourage on-going awareness of security needs
        1. Dealing with disruptive situations
        2. Preventing security breaches
II. Determine time lines for in-service sessions
    A. Incorporate into orientation for new employees; schedule even if there is only one new staff member
    B. Conduct a twice-a-year review and update for all employees
III. Determine contents of training programs for new employees

Manuals, in addition to a training program, are necessary for staff, especially if a problem arises late at night. The security procedures could be included in the departmental manual.

Staff security procedures manual should include at least the following:

1. Telephone numbers
    a. of all staff, with a telephone tree memorandum for calls concerning emergency closing or delayed openings.
    b. of contact individuals for emergencies that occur when library is closed, for police and guard service.
    c. of numbers that should be called if emergencies occur when library is open.
2. List of those authorized to act for the library; also provide a copy of the list to police.
3. Rules and regulations of the library.
4. Guard instructions.
5. Emergency evacuation procedures (including telephone numbers to call, areas of responsibility, location of emergency equipment, evacuation routines); practice ahead of time.
6. Accident report forms and instructions.
7. Incident report forms.
8. Bomb-threat-caller-characteristics form.
9. Civil defense instructions.

10. List of approved vendors (if window is broken).
11. Administrative guidelines.*

Other Security Issues

A library that had a security problem or theft should warn other libraries about thieves in the area. Library hours and geographical location are factors when determining security policies and procedures.

Closing inspection includes checking for electrical devices left on, checking doors and windows, and checking for anyone hiding or asleep in the stacks. Never leave doors unlocked or fail to close them completely. Money should be locked up. A walk-through of the library, with a step-by-step list of what to check, is necessary.

Opening inspection involves doing the opposite of the closing procedure. Turning on lights and equipment, setting up money, and unlocking doors. Again a list in hand is crucial when opening up the library.

You may decide to secure high loss materials by restricting them to reserve, controlled access, reference, or in-house use.

Physical inventory of materials should be taken on a regular basis, so that missing items can be reported promptly.

Security Checklists

Security prevents theft of materials, reduces the rate of loss, physically safeguards materials, and works toward the safety of data and the personal security of staff and patrons. Here are two comprehensive surveys that you may want to modify and use. With many items to consider, a checklist assists you through a security analysis.

Crimin, Wilbur B., "Institutional, Personal, Collection, and Building Security Concern," in Brand, Marvine, ed., Security for Libraries (Chicago: ALA, 1984), pp. 49–50.

Checklist 1 for a Security Survey

1. Security of Collections in All Formats and Equipment
   a. Electronic security system
   b. Closed/restricted collection—access policy
   c. Guards, exit attendants
   d. Publicizing penalties for theft and mutilation
   e. Property stamping, equipment tagging
   f. Current equipment inventory
   g. Equipment storage lockers
   h. Vehicle security and access policy
   i. Proper identification of users or borrowers
   j. After-use procedures to determine damage (if any)
2. Security of Cash
   a. Vending machines: food, photocopiers, card reader dispenser, etc.
   b. Change machines
   c. Access to coin boxes, cash registers
   d. Access to library safe
   e. Cash-handling procedures and accountability
3. Bibliographic and Patron Records
   a. Terminal access, permissions
   b. Passwords
   c. Backup tapes/discs/software
   d. Policy on off-site locations of backup data
   e. Secure storage
4. Personnel Records
   a. Access policy
   b. Supervision of record examination
   c. Use of logs to record access
   d. Policy on removal of confidential documents or other data
   e. Secure storage
5. Employee and Patron Security
   a. Exit and entrance controls
   b. Use of emergency exits
   c. Building design from surveillance point of view

      d. Patrols or television monitors
      e. Building access policy, sign-in
      f. Staff ID badges
      g. Emergency telephones
      h. Outside telephone, emergency
6. Key Policy and Building Security
      a. Procedures for issuing and reclaiming keys
      b. Periodic lock changes
      c. Silent alarms
      d. Parking lot security
      e. Adequate lighting
      f. Custodial services access
      g. Window and bookdrop security
7. Other Considerations
      a. Liability and other types of insurance
      b. Legal counsel provisions
      c. Access to library lawyer for periodic meetings
      d. Budget implications for security measures*

Checklist 2 for a Security Survey

A. Written Security Policies
    1. Explanation of security policies and procedures
    2. Identification of security policies of campus, city, etc.
B. Tour of Physical Facilities
    1. Emergency exits
    2. Parking facilities
    3. Lighting system
    4. Fire alarms
    5. Emergency telephones
    6. Entrances and exits
    7. Restroom security
    8. Special collections requiring additional security
    9. Secluded areas

Thomas W. Shaughnessy. "Security: Past, Present, Future." In Brand, Marvine, ed., Security for Libraries *(Chicago: ALA, 1984), pp. 22–23.*

C. Demonstration of Equipment and Protection Measures
 1. Door locks
 2. Alarm signals, fire drill
 3. Intercom systems
 4. Fire extinguishers
 5. Electronic security and detection systems
 6. First-aid kits
 7. Automatic signaling devices
 8. Pagers, walkie-talkies
 9. Window locks
 10. Money handling
 11. Central control console
 12. Closed-circuit television
D. Major Security Problems and Procedures for Handling
 1. Theft
 2. Mutilation of materials
 3. Nonreturn of materials
 4. Arson
 5. Disruptive patrons
 6. Medical emergencies
 7. Power outages
 8. Bomb threats
 9. Fires, floods, storms
E. Staff's Responsibility
 1. To each other
 2. To the patron
 3. To the collection
F. Auxiliary Personnel
 1. Security guards
 2. City or campus police
 3. Fire department
 4. Paramedics
 5. Mental health and social workers
 6. Legal advisors*

*Paris, Janelle A. "Internal and External Responsibilities and Practices for Library Security." In Brand, Marvine, ed., Security for Libraries (Chicago: ALA, 1984), pp. 80–82.

Besides training, manuals, and checklists you must constantly think about security issues. You should continuously report security problems to your supervisor. Make certain staff fill out report forms. A periodic reevaluation of security policies and procedures with staff participation, especially at meetings, is essential. Let staff bring up their concerns. The posting and dissemination of written existing and revised policies and procedures is a necessary followup to all relevant policy decisions made. Continuously take into account the impact that security measures have on public relations. Get patrons' reactions. How are patrons affected? Do they feel safe? Don't wait until a problem strikes to get patrons' reactions and input.

Set up a review schedule of the mechanical parts of the system. Here are examples of when and what to check:

Electronic detection system, circulation desk—check daily.

Alarm system, both manual and automatic sensor system—check weekly.

Emergency lights—check at least bimonthly.

Battery-operated door alarms—check at least monthly.

Staff security meeting—meet at least once a month.

Fire extinguishers—inspect at least annually.

Fire sensors—check at least biennially.

Security Approaches

Nonelectronic

Nonelectronic approaches to security include closed stacks, security guards, persons checking bags at exits, staff awareness programs, tagged property, cash security, locking doors and windows, closed circuit television cameras, warning signs, lowering the cost of photocopying, and publicity to patrons informing them of the cost and time spent replacing materials. Locking down equipment with steel cables and engraving a identification number on the equipment will help secure materials. Not all of these approaches may be feasible or necessary for your library.

Money sitting around will attract attention. Bank as frequently as possible, and only keep small amounts of petty cash on hand. Stamp checks "For deposit only" as soon as they are received. Make certain that checks are made out to the library or institution and never leave it blank. Money security is stressful. Your organization probably has internal auditing procedures.

Closed circuit television allows staff to monitor what is happening in an area. You may also videotape the action.

So much of security relies on staff. Staff must, for instance, have enough sensitivity to realize they need to watch for patrons who are having difficulty using the library, whose frustration level could thereby lead to theft or mutilation. This alertness allows patrons to know help is available, but also that staff are watching.

Electronic

Many libraries deal with unauthorized removal of materials with the use of electronic systems. A library should consider these points before purchasing an electronic theft detection system:

Some equipment is suitable for monitoring bound books only. Some "targets" (the implanted device that sets off the detection system) are more easily concealed than others and hence more resistant to compromise through tampering. For example, tape targets are more easily concealed than label targets, but they take about four times as long to install. This is because care is needed in inserting tape strip targets to avoid damaging the spine. The sensitivity of alarm systems must be easily adjustable in two directions, to reduce both false alarms and failure to detect targets. Electrical power requirements, space requirements, and the level of maintenance required are all important issues to be considered prior to purchase, along with such questions as, Will it interfere with automated circulation control? Will it harm any materials, video?*

*Morris, John. The Library Disaster Preparedness Handbook. *Chicago:* ALA, 1986; p. 24.

Figure 3.4

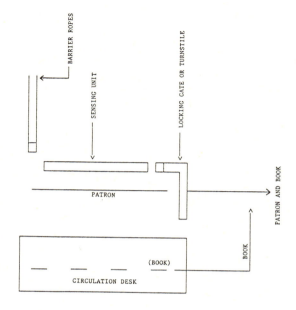

BYPASS METHOD

Figure 3.3

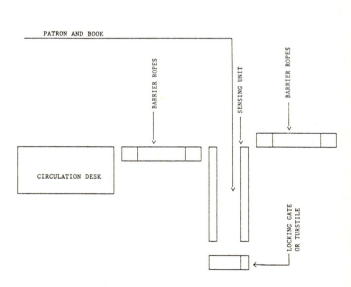

FULL SECURITY METHOD

Electronic security system.

Electronic systems are activated when a sensitized tag concealed in library material, not desensitized in the check out procedure, is taken through a detection field, or when the bypass mode triggers an alarm and a gate or turnstile locks (see Figures 3.3 and 3.4). In the bypass mode, material is inspected by staff and passed around the detection field. There is staff time involved with the tagging of materials.

Libraries have varying policies on how much material "sensitizing" to do: the entire collection, new acquisitions only plus materials that circulate, books only after they have circulated once, software, or art work only.

To avoid detection or to circumvent the system, sometimes patrons throw books out of windows, capitalize on the friendship of desk workers, conceal materials, cut out security tags, orient materials at right angles or hold them above sensors, or sneak out. Test your system periodically to make certain that it is operating. If ordinary library trash is ever taken out via the security system, a tag may trigger the alarm. This may help determine if patrons are cutting out detection tags from materials.

Sometimes you have false alarms or ghost signals which are caused when the system is too near computers. Occasionally, patrons may have something on their person that triggers the alarm, such as a parking garage card. Shields are available for patrons who have something in their purse or wallet that regularly triggers the alarm.

As with any other equipment purchase you must investigate the available products. Attending conference exhibits, reading library literature, and consulting with other libraries should be used in the selection process.

A few words on videotapes. Videotape security is dependent upon a variety of factors that vary with each individual library's ultimate perception of its mission and goals within its community. Likewise work space designs and space utilization must be tailored to each library's specific goals and objectives.*

Some libraries use closed-access shelving with display dummies for video tapes. In this case you need two sets of shelf space and the workload increases for staff. Some libraries use an electronic security system while some libraries do not. Videotapes may be in the open or behind the counter. Other shelving setups include locked cases with staff access only, unlocked cases using commercial boxes as dummy displays, behind the counter access, video browse packs, and the use of security devices to open patron access shelves.

Even though videotape prices are decreasing steadily and the novelty of video is wearing off, is the possibility of any loss acceptable?

Worth keeping in mind are the legal implications of searching for library materials on persons suspected of theft.

*Scholtz, James C., p. 55.

Book return.

Book Return

A book return facility (a "bookdrop") outside the library is a useful piece of equipment that makes it easier for patrons to return materials any hour of the day, possibly saving the patron a fine.

However, there are security problems associated with book returns. You may not want all materials dropped in; for instance, your video- and audiotapes are perhaps not suitable. When software or fragile materials circulate, they may need special containers for protection if your library has a bookdrop. One solution may be to mark in bright colors things not to be put in book returns. Damage may result from materials dropping on top of each other or whenever the temperature is extreme.

Book returns may pose risks, such as fire, when other things besides library materials are dropped. If the book return is in a remote area, you may need to change the return date of the materials. You want to encourage patrons to use them. It is very important to collect the materials on a regular basis. A staff member and a back-up should be trained in collecting the materials.

Book returns on the market, today, lock automatically when full. They also deflect matches, cigarettes, liquid and other harmful material and close automatically. As the unit fills, a suspension system allows a rugged nylon bag to expand, which actually cushions items as they fall.

A spring-loaded platform inside the book return is often best. As more books are deposited the platform gradually goes down.

Confidentiality of Records

In addition to the basic security of materials and patrons, you will also need to be aware of issues surrounding the security of information.

According to the American Library Association's Policy on Confidentiality of Library Records (1971, as revised in 1975, 1986) and in the statement on Professional Ethics, 1981, "Librarians must protect each user's right to privacy with respect to information sought or received and materials consulted, borrowed, or acquired."

Suggested procedures include the following*:

> 1. The library staff member receiving the request to examine or obtain information relating to circulation or other records identifying the names of library users, will immediately refer the person making the request to the responsible officer of the institution, who shall explain the confidentiality policy.
>
> 2. The director, upon receipt of such process, order, or subpoena, shall consult with the appropriate legal officer assigned to the institution to determine if such process, order, or subpoena is in good form and there is a showing of good cause for its issuance.
>
> 3. If the process, order, or subpoena is not in proper form or if good cause has not been shown, insistence shall be made that such defects be corrected before any records are released.
>
> 4. Any threats or unauthorized demands concerning circulation and other records identifying the names of library users shall be reported to the appropriate legal officer of the institution.

*Schmidt, C. James. "Confidentiality of Library Records: Renewed Concerns." Library Administration and Management 2, 4 (1988): 180.

5. Any problems relating to the privacy of circulation and other records identifying the names of library users that are not provided for above shall be referred to the responsible officer. [These guidelines were adopted by the ALA Intellectual Freedom Committee, January 9, 1983, and revised January 11, 1988.]

When a situation arises it may well be the most difficult experience of your career. It is always an emotionally charged issue. Librarians who have faced the confidentiality issue speak of it as a trying experience. Having a policy in effect, legal counsel, and people to back you will lessen the turmoil.

Social Concerns

The Homeless

Libraries are also not exempt from other social concerns. One of the most widespread and common challenges faced by libraries is homelessness. Public buildings and especially public libraries have a long history of dealing with the homeless. The homeless have used public buildings as a place to sleep, to find warm comfortable shelter during cold or rainy weather, to bathe and use restrooms, or to spend the day.

As winter approaches and the temperature dips, the homeless may begin to move into the library. They may bring in their bedding and belongings.

Every town and city has its own way of assisting or not assisting the homeless. Public libraries should recognize the homeless as patrons and not as intruders. Services should be provided to your new patrons.

Latchkey Children

The phenomenon of a latchkey child (one who returns from school to an empty house) is not new although to a great extent its relatively recent impact on middle class families has brought it more into the consciousness of the public. In working class neighborhoods, children have for some time been left on their own while parents worked; the numbers of day care institutions, for instance, only burgeoned with the phenomenon of the second wage-earner in middle class families. Prior to the 1980s some children in ghetto and poor neighborhoods did come into the public library to pass the time, but librarians used other words to describe them and their after-school activities. "Currently, working mothers or single parents of either gender are common in middle-class communities, and the latchkey phenomenon has become institutionalized."*

Public libraries have been viewed by many parents as a safe place for children after school and as an alternative to child care. Unattended or lost preschool children are also common sights in public libraries.

After-school programs have been set up in libraries but the extent of the services depends on funding. Some libraries work in conjunction with local school systems.

If your library does not have a policy on unwanted children or disruptive behavior, adopt one. The policy should clearly define, step by step, appropriate actions. Patrons, parents, and staff will know what is expected of them. The policy will protect kids and lower stress among staff. The "What do I do now" response will disappear.

Summary

Libraries must remain committed to providing access to their materials and services for all users. Patron records must be kept confidential. Thefts and mutilations will always be problems, no matter what policies are pursued by your library. No controls are completely effective. Patrons who are determined to steal or mutilate materials will succeed. The most you can do is remain observant and use whatever controls seem practical for your library.

---

*Naylor, Alice Phoebe. "Reaching All Children: A Public Library Dilemma." Library Trends 35, 3 (1987): 384.

Libraries are and should always remain relatively clean, safe, and healthy places to work, study and spend free time. You must actively encourage among your staff a greater awareness of their surroundings and discourage in them any complacent feelings of security. Libraries are located in prisons, inner cities, small towns, rural areas, universities, corporations, schools, hospitals, high rises, suburbs, zoos, and museums—and every location has its own concerns.

4
Stack Management

The Computer

Marge works on her five year stack plan. Traditionally, her library only collected books but lately videotapes and microfilm are slowly entering the circulating collection. She now considers where and how to store them when managing the stacks.

As Marge works, she suddenly realizes that just one year ago, her calculations and reports were done using a calculator and typewriter. Previously, she dreaded this time of year and the task but not this year. Today, she sits at the department computer and runs the in-house-use data through Lotus 1-2-3, a statistical software package. At the touch of a key, a graph comparing monthly photocopy statistics and in-house use is printed. Now with the computer, Marge spends more time working with her staff and on special projects. Just the other day a bat was swooping on patrons, but that is another story...

Introduction

Stack management is the process of planning, organizing, and controlling materials in the library stacks, and leading the personnel who administer them. This chapter introduces the concept of planning and suggests ways to make planning productive. Planning is every librarian's job: before you can organize or lead, you must make plans to accomplish the job. To be an effective manager, you must delegate essential tasks to others and coordinate the efforts of your individual workers.

Stack management could be deemed the critical function of access services. In large collections, a misshelved book is in many cases as good as lost. It may be many years before shelf-reading of the stacks turns it up, and in the meantime, money may have been spent searching for and replacing it.

The author's experience has been that the "not-on-shelf" situation is the number one cause of patron frustration and anger. The second source of frustration is the nonworking photocopier. No matter what the source, you must aggressively manage the stacks in order to reduce patron frustration.

Whatever the arrangement of materials, size of the collection, or format, accessibility is the essential element. Access and ease of use enhance the value of any library material. Accessibility depends upon the accurate and timely placement of materials.

Librarians must face stack issues daily. Some libraries shelve journals alphabetically while other libraries order journals by call numbers. Are patrons able to retrieve their own materials or does library staff page the materials? Materials may be housed on the premises or off-site. No matter how your materials are arranged, if patrons cannot locate desired materials then the library has no practical value to them. Stack assistance for patrons is mandatory to guide them through the diversity of library arrangements.

What has been technology's impact on the stacks? The fundamental principle of shelving materials has not been replaced. Materials must be returned to the shelves and kept in order. Returning materials to the shelves is still the number one priority. The nonshelving of materials interferes with the rights of the patron. It is extremely difficult to envision any library where the physical placement of materials will not take place. Certainly some kinds of technology, such as facsimile or computers, may make your job easier; stack maintenance, however, involves labor intensive work. The staff makes the stack operation succeed or fail. This element affects all of your plans and efforts.

Besides shelving responsibilities, stack management facilitates collection development. With the increasing price of journal subscriptions, monographs and other materials, use studies have become significant for collection development. Front line preservation techniques can also be practiced during routine stack maintenance.

Maintaining the stacks is much more than the shelving of materials, as you will soon discover after reading this chapter. Let's start with a brief review of materials found in libraries.

Materials

First of all, libraries house much more than books, newspapers, or journals. Materials such as software, compact discs, microforms, audio- and videotapes, records, toys, games, classroom notes, art prints, globes, audiovisual equipment, theses and dissertations, artifacts, skeletons, learning tools, film strips, slides, movies, or photographs must all be arranged and shelved for easy access. An academic library might subscribe to scientific research journals while the neighborhood public library has the latest do-it-yourself plumbing book. Demand exists for all materials.

An integrated collection makes nonprint materials equal partners. In this time of changing formats, you must apply the concept of equality to all library materials. Books are no longer the only sources of information.

Considering the diversity of materials, it is not surprising that there are a great variety of library stack arrangements. For example, in academic libraries the shelving preference of nonprint materials appears to be by format.

Will patrons have direct access to materials? Are patrons able to browse the collections or must they request titles? Will your stack workers page the materials? Will you integrate all formats? For any material, access issues include:

The stacks.

1. Location. Where will it go? Modify existing, as is, in library or shelve off-site?
2. Security, protection.
3. Additional needs: for example, for software is a computer nearby or available, do you need special equipment or supplies, new book trucks?
4. Policies, procedures.
5. Copyright.
6. Staffing. What will staff be responsible for? Are there any special services or training issues?
7. Publicity. Location handouts. How do patrons know where to look?

Collection Arrangement

Unless you are starting or completely revising a library collection, the arrangement of materials in your stacks is already established. It can be said, though, that no library is ever truly finished. It is important to acknowledge the possible appearance of new formats. Circulating software for patron use was not a reasonable consideration ten years ago. An awareness of this should trigger your keeping an eye on the library literature for upcoming trends. You cannot effectively manage the stacks functioning in a vacuum.

Journal articles usually discuss stack arrangements with studies of particular systems or reports of the experiences from individual institutions—the "how *we* did it" approach. The justification of this apparently narrow approach is based on the belief that every library has different policies or philosophies concerning collections, materials, shelving arrangements, and service. It is impossible to create one perfect arrangement under these circumstances.

No one solution is best for every library. My answer to your shelving problems may be too costly, physically impossible, or politically suicidal for your library. Arrangements must be designed to fit the distinct characteristics of the library. Simply put, no two libraries are identical. Fortunately, there are similar factors to consider when organizing the stacks. You can gain insights from the literature.

Your circulation policies directly affect the physical arrangement of the materials. For example, if software or videotapes have restrictive use then the software or videotapes should not be shelved in open stacks, but kept in a staff controlled area. When materials circulate, stack workers should handle those materials upon their return.

Sorting areas for arranging materials in proper order prior to being shelved are critical to efficient shelving. Although space limitations may prevent the ideal arrangement of the materials, you must nevertheless make every attempt to optimize your stack space.

Closed Stacks

Is the library using or will it use compact shelving because of stack growth problems? The stacks may be closed to protect rare materials or to control materials, or because of tightly packed stacks. Closed stacks require the paging of materials. How quickly will you be able to fill the requests? There will be less misshelving in closed stacks. Shelf-reading becomes less of a responsibility when only staff touch the materials in the stacks, especially when the staff are well trained.

During the course of the work day, how will contact with the staff be made regarding requests? Will you use a beeper system? If some of the material is at a remote location, you need to inform patrons how often a retrieval run occurs.

Open Stacks

Open stacks eliminate the need for paging but the amount of shelf-reading, searching and monitoring, and stress on the collection all increase. In open stacks, patrons have direct access to the materials. You must remind patrons not to reshelve their materials but to leave them in designated areas. The job of collecting, sorting, and reshelving materials is easier when you provide a number of collection points where patrons can leave items.

Classification System

Classification systems, Dewey Decimal or Library of Congress, make subject browsing of materials possible. In public libraries, fiction may be arranged in alphabetical order according to the author's last name. Fiction collection(s) may also first be ordered as to genre—science fiction, detective, western, romances, mysteries, etc.—or by audience—children, young adult, adult, and so on. Academic libraries classify fiction as "literature," and both literature as well as nonfiction are arranged by call number.

Figure 4.1

Example of rules for shelving word-by-word

(1) Titles are arranged according to the alphabetical sequence of their significant words.

Initial articles; and *internal articles, conjunctions and prepositions* (in any language) are ignored for shelving purposes.

Examples:

AARBOK for UNIVERSITETET i BERGEN

ABHANDLUNGEN zur GESCHICHTE der
   NATURWISSENSCHAFTEN

ABSTRACTS of BACTERIOLOGY

JOURNAL d'UROLOGIE

VIERTELJAHRSSCHRIFT für GERICHTLICHE

VORTRAGE aus der PRAKTISCHEN CHIRURGIE

Articles to be disregarded in shelving of titles, if they occur at the beginning of the title [examples only]:

Arabic: al-, el-, ad-, ar-, as-, at-, az-

Dutch: de, het, 't, een, enne

English: the, a, an

Common articles, conjunctions and prepositions to be disregarded when occurring internally in a title [examples only]:

a, and, auf, by, d', da, de, de la, dem, der, di, e, et, for, from, für, gli, on, the, und

(2) When a *conjunction* or a *preposition* precedes the first significant word in the title, it is considered a significant word.

Example:

IN VITRO

(3) Initialisms and acronyms are treated as words:

Example:

BMJ

JAMA

JCU Journal of Clinical Ultrasound

NIEUWE NEDERLANDSE

A call number subject bookmark assists patrons in remembering where a subject is shelved.

Journals may also be arranged according to a classification system. Bound periodicals are classified and intershelved with the main collections.

Alphabetical Arrangement

Some journal collections are alphabetically organized. Most people believe that an alphabetization based on a word-by-word principle makes shelving of materials simpler for staff and easier for patrons to find materials; some believe in letter-by-letter (i.e., the way most computers nowadays do it). Bound journals are shelved by title in a segregated alphabetical sequence. You need rules to follow when training the shelving staff. In Figure 4.1, certain words are ignored when shelving word-by-word.

When journals are arranged alphabetically, patrons can walk through the stacks with a computer search printout and find their journal materials without having to go to a catalog for the appropriate call number.

Other Issues

Government documents require special attention and present their own shelving complexities. How will you arrange the materials? By Superintendent of Documents number? Catalogers must do the classifying and cataloging of materials, but herein lies another opportunity to interact with technical services.

Will you have totally integrated shelving arrangements, regardless of format? Scanning a shelf filled with plastic video cases, metal film cans, or microform boxes is hardly as rewarding as browsing among print collections. Nonprint arrangements differ from library to library.

Videotape shelving arrangement should (1) facilitate ease of browsing and title locations, (2) be organized in a way that is readily apparent to patrons, and (3) be kept as simple as possible but with subject/genre areas sufficiently delineated to avoid

The periodical room.

confusion. These factors are applicable to any format arrangement.

The patron plays a role in stack arrangements. Are certain materials, such as those with sex or drug themes, dissertations, or rare books, kept locked? If the patrons are elementary school children you must take a hard look at the physical access of the arrangements. Can the materials be comfortably reached? No matter what the arrangement, it should be based on ease of access for the patron.

Ease of Access

The ease of finding materials must be included in the stack arrangement. Again, shelving arrangements should facilitate ease of browsing and finding title locations, be organized in a logical manner and be kept as simple as possible.

You may have an intricate stack scheme but if staff or patrons spend hours searching for an item, is it worth it? What have you accomplished but staff and patron frustration?

What about a change in journal title? New materials are continually being added while superseded or less-used materials are being withdrawn. When the journal collection is ordered by call numbers, title changes are easier to shelve. You do not need to shelve volumes of a particular journal separately when titles change because classification does not change. An alphabetical arrangement usually requires volumes of a journal to be shelved separately whenever a title change occurs. For example, the original title of a journal is *Journal of Occupational Medicine* but if the title changes to *JOM*, with an alphabetical arrangement the new and old titles are not shelved next to each other.

You must do something to guide staff and patrons. Dummies for location or title changes may be made of wood, paper, or plastic. The dummies may be booklike in appearance or just a flat piece of cardboard. No matter what is used, the dummies must be kept in order. Aisle indexes may help patrons locate materials in the stacks but must be maintained and kept up to date. Range finders in the stacks are necessary. As patrons enter the stacks, they need a frame of reference, even with a map in hand. In a large stack area the patron is often bewildered and disoriented by row after row of ranges. Guide to the classification scheme and each shelf or range of shelves should be clearly labelled to show where to find materials.

Special shelving requirements for oversized materials exist. Oversized materials may not fit on conventionally sized shelving but may need wider shelving and may even need to be separated from the regular collection.

Displays

Arrangements for display of books, newspapers, new materials, currently received journals, toys, theses, and microforms must be maintained. There are display units available for all materials. How new is new? What will you display? Constantly rotating the collection takes staff time. What will be accessible to patrons? You must clarify how and for how long the materials will be displayed before relocating them to the stacks.

There are good-looking cases which clearly display video-tapes so titles are easy to spot. Cases, with or without locking doors, feature sloping shelves that enable tape covers or spines to be pulled out for convenient browsing and selection. Locking compact disc display cases and record display units exist. News-papers can be displayed on slanted shelves or on sticks. Display units exist for every format—the choices are nearly endless.

Unbound Versus Bound Journals

Unbound journals need to be controlled differently from bound journals. Will unbound journal issues be shelved with their respective bound counterparts? A periodical room allows current periodicals to be separated in order to facilitate their use. This ready access to periodicals on open shelves encourages browsing of the materials. The materials may be arranged according to subject, call number, or title.

Many libraries have found that keeping new issues separate for a week, or until the next issue arrives, encourages the patron to come into the library on a regular basis. Or you may keep all that arrive Monday together throughout the week.

Unbound current issues should be kept together, and it is better not to send the latest volume to the bindery until the first issue of the next volume has been received. Stacks are easier to maintain when unbounds are separate from the bound arrangement. Magazines, periodicals, and journals all refer to the material type.

A wide variety of shelving for periodicals (e.g. with open shelves or flip-up panels) exists, making access easier.

Bindery

When materials are in process for the bindery, where will the materials be held? Will patrons have access to the materials until the materials leave the library? Will you charge out materials to the bindery?

Patrons must be kept aware of any temporary changes in the location of materials. For example, when material is sent to a bindery, patrons need to know that the material is unavailable.

There are many other issues to consider when managing the stacks. Sometimes materials need to be safeguarded in acid-free boxes, loose-leaf binders, or acid-free pamphlet envelopes. Can these special boxes be maintained in open stacks? Appropriate equipment is needed to move, protect, organize and plan your collections.

Are All Book Trucks Created Equal?

Stack equipment includes book trucks, shelves, bookends, ladders or step stools, flood kit, water vacuum, dust vacuum, fans, and a personal computer. These basic items are imperative for managing the stacks.

An up-to-date inventory list of departmental supplies and equipment is useful in any number of situations. For example, when justifying the purchase of new equipment, compiling a report, or reordering supplies, such a list will save you time.

Many companies specialize in the library market. Just take a look through the many catalogs available. As you examine any one of the catalogs you may feel like a kid in a candy store. New equipment, however, may be expensive. For example, a book truck, today, costs over $300. Before purchasing any item, even if the cost appears inexpensive, you should investigate all options. You should attempt to obtain product evaluations and see in person what you are buying. A quick reference phone call to another library could save you money, aggravation, and time. I feel that most people are willing to discuss their positive or negative equipment experiences. Someday you may be on the receiving end of a call.

Your organization most likely has budgetary limitations and restrictions. Someone else probably controls your purse strings; however by researching the product you will have a more convincing case for your choices.

A book truck.

Book Trucks

Each library has limitations set by its physical environment. The selection of an inappropriate book truck could leave the library sounding like a bowling alley. Numerous book trucks, all-terrain, metal, wood, and audiovisual carts, are available on the market. Each truck fills a particular library requirement and environment. In addition, weight and size of materials to be transported need to be factored into the selection process. For example, consider small trucks for easier maneuverability and safety. Oversized items need larger trucks with deep shelves.

You must also look at the physical conditions the shelvers and trucks face during the course of a workday. Are there any stairs to negotiate within the library? Are materials shelved off-site? What will the trucks be used for and who will use them? Are the floor surfaces smooth, tiled, carpeted, or bumpy? Each surface requires a different size and type of book truck wheel and shaft.

Equipment wears out or finds its way out of the library. Will you refurbish your book trucks or purchase replacement trucks? What about wheel replacement? Unfortunately, nothing lasts forever. You must plan for future equipment needs.

Shelving

The selection process for shelving can be complicated and frustrating. Take a field trip to a library that uses the shelving that interests you. When attending conferences talk with colleagues and vendors. It will probably be impossible to have an exact match with any older shelving. If children's materials are interfiled remember to consider the height of shelving. When the patrons are small children, they have different shelf height requirements than an adult. Again, we return to the patron. Also, you must decide how much of your shelving will be used for oversized materials. Get out there and see your choices in action. Do not forget bookends. The bookend should be given careful attention.

Bookends

The apparently modest bookend can make a staff's life easier and a book's life longer. How laborious will it be using that bookend? In the marketplace, you will find metal book supports with plain, composition cork, urethane, or felt bases, plastic book supports with bases, or wire book supports. Tall and short bookends exist. The selection process for appropriate bookends involves consideration of the shelves, ease of use by patrons and staff, and, possibly, aesthetic needs.

Miscellaneous

Also, ladders, step stools, vacuums (dust and water) are all valid equipment selections. A water vacuum is one item you

The step stool, and step ladder.

want to have on hand but hope you never need to use. Vacuums for material, equipment, and computer cleaning are justified because of their preventive maintenance capability. How high are the stacks? How will materials on the top shelf be reached? You do not want anyone using the shelves as ladders. Step stools and ladders are necessities.

Personal Computers

On the other cost extreme, a personal computer system and appropriate software eliminate piles of paper, speed up processes, and decrease errors. The benefit of the computer is that the processing and creating of paperwork is done with greater accuracy and speed. With software programs, you can retrieve statistical data or print graphs with the stroke of a key.

In addition to being an aid to your projects, the computer

should be perceived and treated as a staff development tool, preparing staff for higher positions. This may be a staff's first exposure to computers. Thus, by using a computer to achieve your own projects, you also encourage staff to further develop their skills.

Should you use an IBM, a personal computer clone, or a Macintosh? The "which is better" debate rages on. Each computer serves different needs and audiences. Ask yourself, "What do I want it for?" The computers require different operating systems and hardware so check around with other users. Although the preference for either IBM or Macintosh is an unusually emotional issue, the real conflict is a matter of personal taste rather than the clear superiority of one over the other. The difference between IBM'ers and Mac'ers is subjective. You will get plenty of advice, do not worry. You must learn what computers others in the library use because compatibility will be imperative for the sharing of information, compiling of statistics, or the creation of newsletters, reports, and signs. The DOS-Mac connection possibilities are dulling down the sharp differences between IBM and Macintosh.

The Macintosh has slowly been finding its way into all types of libraries to handle many traditional computing tasks, such as online searching and some circulation functions, and also new jobs, such as desktop publishing and hypercard guide tours. These machines are being used as interactive tools to communicate with other Macintoshes, personal computers, microcomputers, and mainframes.

Don't forget the printer. Production of hard copy is essential for word processing, data reports, sign making, and spreadsheets. Because it is the component with the largest number of mechanical parts, the printer tends to have more maintenance problems.

A dot matrix character is produced by forcing a rigid and limited array of printed dots into the shape of the selected character. The quality of the print depends on the number of printing pins located in the print head, which sets the character used by the printer. Dot matrix printers are cheap, rugged, and all-purpose. The 24-pin type can produce fairly decent output. Laser printers yield the best results, but they are a good deal more expensive than dot matrix printers. There are also ink-jet printers available. The quality is good, but not great. Again, you must research printers and look at the compatibility issue. If you will be producing newsletters, flyers, or notices, the laser printer is wonderful.

A surge protector, locks, and a tool kit are additional mandatory items. Security must be your first concern. You need general purpose software packages such as word processors, data management, spreadsheets, and graphics. Explore software packages as carefully as you researched the computer. Without well-chosen software, the computer will remain untouched.

Software: Key to Success

First, determine the needs your computer will fulfill for access services. For example, will its uses include compiling statistics, word processing, desktop publishing, handouts, database management, sign making, or communications? Ways of exploring software include asking your coworkers or peers, personal hands-on experience, visiting a computer store, and investigating your institution's computer support center (if you are lucky enough to have one) or resident expert.

The way to maneuver safely through this product maze is by researching the product. When selecting software, scan pertinent computer journals for software reviews. For example, read *MacUser* or *MacWorld* for Macintosh software reviews. Various equipment and software review guides are published today. *Library Technology Reports* comes out six times a year; each issue covers a library equipment topic in depth. For example, one issue was devoted to use of personal computers for circulation functions. Other useful sources are *Byte, PC World, PC Magazine, PC Digest,* and *Software Review.* Because the field of personal computing changes quickly, journals are the best source of current information on software and computers.

You should be wary of new or unproven products. If a product review speaks of minor problems, a red warning flag should go up. Probably more hidden problems in the software exist so it is best to wait.

Once you have purchased the software there are also things to consider. First, it is important to make backup copies of all important programs and data files. Keep the original and one backup in fire-resistant, dust-proof, protective containers. Day-to-day entry should be done on backup copies.

Software programs are assigned release numbers by the developers to indicate the version of the program. When the developer makes significant changes to the software and issues a new release, the software has been upgraded. Inevitably you will need to upgrade your software. Software programs are constantly being improved and expanded. Vendors try to make revisions as easy as possible, but changing from one version to an upgraded version is disruptive.

When chosen properly, the software will prove beneficial when you start entering data and text and start printing your first report or graph. If you already use a particular software program, ask yourself, is it being used to its full potential? You may soon realize that the perfect software program does not exist for your application but you may be able to modify the existing software to fit your needs.

A modem makes it possible for the computer to communicate with another computer by using the telephone system. Communication software and a modem allow access to electronic mail, document requests, database searching, and the expanding information world.

Electronic Spreadsheet

Spreadsheet software has much to offer in the management of the stacks. A spreadsheet is a grid that allows you to sort and recalculate any computed cells. You need to design the layout of the spreadsheet to fit your needs. You might have developed a

Figure 4.2
Shelving Activities

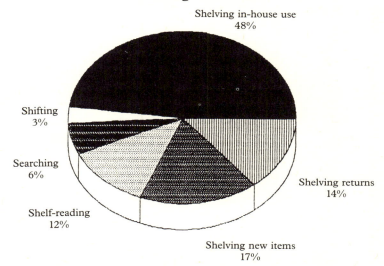

Shelving in-house use
48%

Shifting
3%

Searching
6%

Shelf-reading
12%

Shelving returns
14%

Shelving new items
17%

useful format on paper that would serve your electronic needs. You must always ask yourself, for what purpose are these data being collected? Spreadsheet software is useful for analyzing highly variable data. (See Figures 4.2, 4.3, and 4.4.) Library collections are very dynamic, with everything having a different rate of growth and new material added while less-used materials are withdrawn. The spreadsheet allows you to make sense of the data and determine "what if." You can manipulate the data and examine different scenarios.

Don't be number happy—have specific uses for the data. Think about what is important. Many hours and much expense go into collecting information. Analyze your data and use them for decision making or problem solving.

The collection of data allows you to determine the cost of tasks, determine the use of materials, compile an inventory of materials, and discover use patterns. Effective managing requires the analysis of up-to-date data. You cannot make future plans using two-year-old information. Stack workers provide the necessary assistance for collecting the data.

Figure 4.3
Photocopies vs ILL (not on shelf)

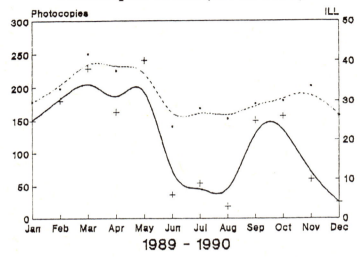

Photocopies in thousands

Figure 4.4
Photocopies vs Computer Searches

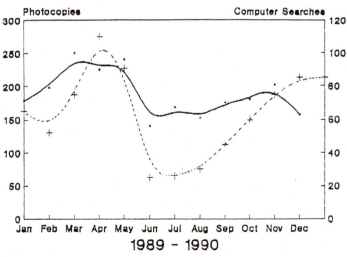

Photocopies in thousands

Figure 4.5
Example of a spreadsheet:

```
Journal Inventory
```

Number	NG/G	Title	Existing Bound Ft	Inches	5YR	10YR
1.	G	AANA Journal	2.00	9.00		
2.	NG	AAOHN		2.50		
3.	G					

Spreadsheet programs are a classic one-time investment. Once you learn how to use one, you will be reluctant to change, so consider buying the most flexible program. In many cases, the price difference between spreadsheet programs is not substantial, so the initial investment in a high-end product will ensure that you have plenty of room for growth.

Lotus 1-2-3 is a DOS-based spreadsheet package with a wide range of practical applications, from budgeting to inventory to scheduling classes to tracking productivity. Version 2.01 has been the industry spreadsheet standard for three years. A new version of Lotus is now available. (See Figure 4.5.) Quatro Pro is another spreadsheet program receiving rave reviews.

Growth

Growth space is provided on the shelf, in the section, or in the range. Various formulas for determining growth rates of materials are available. How much space should be left on a shelf? You may know your collections, but it is still difficult to determine growth or forecast variable collections.

Two common practices allowing for growth without major shifting are the setting up of shelving without using top and bottom shelves, and with blank ranges or shelves periodically spaced. Leaving space after each journal title based on amount and size of previous years is another method, but remember that journals grow, change titles, cease, or start up. In 1992, a title may be five volumes instead of four. If a journal has been discontinued, you can then condense space. With monographs you may only use half to three-quarters of the shelf, leaving the remainder for growth. It all depends on your stack capacity (85 percent is usually considered full).

Some basic definitions may be in order now. The *capacity* of an area is its total linear feet of shelving. *Linear feet* is the standard of measurement used in the determination of shelf space and in computing the size of a collection. A *section* is a vertical arrangement of shelves, normally consisting of a base shelf and shelves of approximately 35 inches in length. A *single-faced range* is a row of sections.

Material Move

Sometimes because of lack of growth space you must plan for a material move. With the spreadsheet program, you can manipulate the data and investigate all possibilities. A move may occur at any time for any reason; therefore preparation is necessary.

The Yale University Medical Library, from 1988 to 1990, underwent renovation and construction while still providing full access to the collection and photocopiers. The collections were constantly being shifted; the possibility existed that at any time construction needs would require us to move it again with minimum delay. The shelves in some areas were so crowded that materials were lined up on the floor as well as shelved in awkward nooks and corners. Constant shifting became the norm. On occasion, we had to shift many shelves of materials in order to replace a couple of volumes.

Your collections are not static but exist within two changing environments: the informational and the physical. Before doing any moving, do the following:

1. Measure the collection. Calculate the approximate size of the collection to be moved. Once you have the spreadsheet developed, the numbers can easily be inserted and manipulated.
2. Look at what is available in terms of equipment, staff, and money.
3. Determine the amount of available shelf space.

4. Decide how you want the collection to be laid out—where the starting point will be.

5. Plan the move step by step. Make sure everything is ready and set a timetable. If an elevator is crucial to the move, have it thoroughly checked out to make sure it is working properly.

6. Prepare areas and materials. Shelf-read and house-clean prior to the move. Mark shelves if necessary. Moving rare books requires care in physical handling, accuracy in the control of records, and adequate security to prevent loss or damage. Merging different collections or groups in advance of the move will ultimately save you time. Blending small collections into the general collection during the move may be your only option.

7. If a moving company will be doing the actual work, meet with them beforehand. Train the movers. Also, have at least one staff member monitor them. You will need someone there, no matter how many hours are spent discussing the job and establishing a working relationship.

If library staff does the move, do you have enough equipment? Will you rent or borrow additional equipment? Will you need to hire temporary workers?

Shelf-reading the collection before, during, and after the move is the only way to be certain materials are in order.

You need to sit, plan, and think before rushing into any action. The goal is not to do it again but to do it right the first time.

Collection Development Connection

Circulating materials produce only a portion of the data on collection use. In-house use statistics and materials picked up from reader stations and photocopy areas provide extremely significant data. In-house use statistics quantify the browsing, studying, or recreational use of materials. Unfortunately, such data are troublesome to calculate precisely. You must also, for instance, subtract periodical issues received, bindery returns, new materials, or returned books from total shelving activity to obtain accurate statistics.

A variety of methods are available for measuring in-house statistics. Sampling often gives reliable results: look at a small, average sample and taking the results to represent the entire project. Use a table of random numbers to determine the work days for data collection. Select the days to sample, take a sample of work days and collect the data. You could use the sampling technique to count two days a month, count every day, or use automation techniques. For example, when materials are barcoded you could electronically read the barcodes of material to be shelved. If your collection is small or you have a large staff, you may do a daily count of the materials per truck/shelf.

Libraries purchase limited amounts of materials because of budget and space restrictions. Knowing the collection's use effectively guides decision making. With in-house statistics at your fingertips you can learn how to further facilitate the use of the collection, and ultimately you can provide valid use numbers to collection development. These in-house numbers, along with circulation (out of library use) or loan numbers, assist collection development decisions with the cancellation of titles, weeding of materials, and the selection of new titles. When decisions are made with valid numbers all the guesswork disappears. Who else is in a better position to measure collection use than the stack worker, who handles the materials daily.

A component to the deselection process may be to tag targeted materials with their costs and then follow up with a questionnaire for patrons. Patron involvement tests the political climate and lessens any backlash that may occur with cancellations.

Do not hesitate to offer sincere support and good numerical data to technical services and collection development people. Access services must assertively demonstrate its contribution to the library.

Do You Work Here?

Anything assisting patrons in finding materials will make everyone's life better. A handout of the stack arrangements expedites patrons in their pursuit of materials but only to a certain point. Your staff must be prepared to answer questions in addition to maintaining the materials in order.

The key to excellent stack service is the stack team. When a staff member works in the stacks, a patron will usually ask him or her for help. Interaction with stack staff, especially during evening and weekend hours, may be the only direct contact patrons have with the library. Stack staff do provide reference service.

The highly visible stack staff should know the collections' idiosyncrasies and probable trouble areas. A useful rule would be to treat the patron the way that you would like to be treated.

One way to build team spirit and help patrons find materials is the wearing of FINDER buttons or FINDER hats (or FINDER "whatever") by the staff. This FINDER image will readily identify whom to ask for assistance. This also creates a special identity for staff to rally around.

Sometimes patrons or stack staff are not able to find materials on the shelves; therefore you need a mechanism for locating missing materials. An effective search procedure requires time-lines and a conclusion to the process. Others will need to know the outcome of the search. For example, set a standard to explain results (see Figure 4.6). If you have many searches, staff cannot possibly remember every outcome.

The search process requires verification of call number and ownership, and a determination whether it is checked out, for repair, at the bindery, or at an alternative location like the new book section. Whenever possible it is best to search for the material when the patron is present but in most cases that is impossible. If the material is determined to be lost you must decide whether to order a replacement. Searching can be a major expense, especially for libraries with open stacks.

Figure 4.6
Stack Section
Searching Abbreviations
Explanations

TNOS	Title not on shelf
VNOS	Volume/issue not on shelf
DNOT	Do not own title
DNOV	Do not own volume
BNDRY	Bindery
CIT	Wrong citation; where you checked: EX: 01984, 0 v.6
MSG	Missing/on search
NYR	Not yet received
IN USE	Charged out
IN PROC	Being processed
REORD	Reorder material
HD/RC	Put on hold or recall

The Stacks

The Human Factor

Preservation and conservation in libraries are ideas whose time has come. Academic libraries throughout the country are creating preservation departments and hiring conservators.

Libraries are filled with book and nonbook materials made of chemically unstable materials which are housed in polluted atmospheres under changing conditions of temperature and humidity. It is imperative that all library planning include preservation as an important consideration.

Public libraries are also facing the preservation challenge.

> It has been easy for public librarians to assume that their collections are expendable, that maintenance need be minimal, and that problems of deteriorating books can be solved by larger acquisition budgets and more aggressive weeding. Yet public

libraries cannot escape the preservation problems that affect all collections. Public libraries may need the service of a preservation consultant.*

In one study of public library materials, adult fiction was found to be in the poorest condition. These materials are newer but are heavily used by the public and frequently returned through the bookdrop. The bindings of books today are of poor quality and do not last long with heavy use.†

Typically, academic libraries are committed to preserving all materials. Public libraries have a different focus and must think of long-term implications, the nature of materials, and shelf life.

Nationwide efforts are underway to preserve the deteriorating books in our libraries. All this has come about because of the realization that all is not well in our library stacks. The stack staff performs a preservation role for the library.

Pamela Darling, a preservation specialist at Columbia University, in speaking at a conference on "Library Preservation: Implementing Programs" in 1985, described the factors that are causing these problems in the stacks:

> Factors affecting library materials deterioration include: 1. intrinsic factors, such as materials which self-destruct due to their inherent acidity; 2. factors in the physical environment, such as reactant atmospheric pollutants and inappropriate and destructive storage; 3. human experimental factors, such as careless handling and care by staff and patrons.

This section focuses on the third factor, the human factor, and developing sound training programs for teaching stack maintenance to employees. By contrast, the articles in the various library periodicals that mention stack maintenance usually discuss stack cleaning, environmental controls, and stack lighting at greater length than the activities of the staff.

Reynolds, Anne L., Schrock, Nancy C., and Walsh, Joanna. "Preservation: The Public Library Response." Library Journal 114, 3 (1989): 128.

†*Reynolds, Anne L., pp. 128–132.*

Granted these physical concerns are extremely important for the proper care of library materials, but careless or poorly trained stack maintenance staff can undo many of the efforts of the preservation work and can negate a clean and controlled stack environment. Stack staff positions tend to be entry level, making training a necessity. Training is the key to a successful stack program.

Training

How to achieve good stack maintenance habits in stack workers is not generally addressed in the literature. A good place to begin is with the compilation of a stack manual tailored to a particular library's stack needs. This manual should be distributed and explained to every staff member. A training sheet checklist should be included in the manual, assuring that all training questions are addressed and providing a record of training for later reference. (See Figure 4.7.)

The manual should include how to shelve, how to retrieve books, how to photocopy materials, how to shelf-read, and how to care for books that are in poor condition. Possibly, the manual could include a stack shelving pretest and a posttest. Reminders of safety issues, such as the use of a step stool and not the shelving to reach high stacks, or care when lifting or pushing book trucks, are never a waste of time.

Along with the how-to directions, include emergency procedures and phone numbers. The manual might also include citations to pertinent articles on preservation and relevant sections from books on preservation, that would be kept in a staff-only part of the library. For example, good drawings of the anatomy of the book in Jane Greenfield's *Books: Their Care and Repair* (H.W. Wilson, 1983) can help staff become familiar with the physical parts of books and learn where the stress or weak spots of books are located. Staff who know about hinges and text blocks will be more likely to keep books upright on shelves and book trucks.

Initial training programs for staff should include a display

Figure 4.7
Training Sheet
Stacks

NAME_____

DATE_____

SIGN IN
Time Slips _____
Truck Log _____
Daily Worksheets _____
Book Count Log _____
Manual _____

PHOTOCOPY PICKUPS:
Room _____
Loan Desk _____

SORTING
Bounds _____
Unbounds _____
Monographs _____
Reference _____
Reserve _____

SHELVING
Journals _____
Monographs _____
Reference _____
Oversize _____

COLLECTION MAINTENANCE
Stack sweeps _____
Lighting _____
Shelf reading _____
Shifting _____
Problem report _____

PHOTOCOPY MACHINES
Meter readings _____
Add paper _____
Add dry ink _____
Clear jams _____
Change waste bottle _____
Cleaning _____
Problem reports _____
Card boxes/changing _____

DOCUMENT DELIVERY
Facsimile _____
Blue slips _____

EMERGENCY PROCEDURES
Phone list _____
Manual _____

of maimed books—that is, books that have had the misfortune to be mishandled. Demonstrations on the proper methods for removing books from the shelves and photocopying can be reinforced by exhibiting books with torn spines caused by improper handling.

You may decide to create a preservation awareness workshop, possibly in conjunction with a group of local libraries, using slides or videotape. It would work well when training staff or increasing the awareness of patrons. Also, you may decide to use this standardized program on the road, in area libraries, schools, or at community events.

A well trained, preservation-conscious stack staff will perform good stack maintenance and keep the collections in serviceable condition. It frequently means more work for the supervisor in that more time must be spent in designing training programs and in doing the actual training, but well planned training is well worth the time!

Shelf-Reading

Shelf-reading, the art of keeping the collections in correct order, is a wonderful opportunity to get stack staff concerned with the collection in their care. Relevant factors as to how fast staff can shelf-read are the size of each volume and the amount of space it occupies on the shelf. If a volume is not thick enough to have a call number on the spine, the shelf-reader must partially remove the item in order to confirm the location, slowing down the work. Shelf-reading can also be affected by the amount of free space available.

At first glance, shelf-reading appears to be a boring task but if it's expanded into a preservation review as well as an order review it can become an interesting and rewarding job.

The stack staff should start shelf-reading armed with a shelf-reading log (see Figure 4.8) to keep track of the work accomplished and any special problems encountered. For example, call numbers of books in poor condition can be recorded and a list of these items kept for further action. The overcrowded

Figure 4.8
Stack Section
Shelf-Reading Log

Area Assigned _____/_____

Title/Call #	Shelforder	Edging	Sweeping	Bookends	Tight fit

Name _____ Date _____

Starting time _____ am pm

Finishing time _____ am pm

Total time _____hrs _____ min

shelving sections can also be noted for later shifting. The shelf-reader should be equipped with binding string and scissors. Books with damaged covers or with loose pages can be tied up to keep all the parts together until permanently repaired. A supply of acid-free pamphlet envelopes and boxes should also be on hand. Old, crumbling, acidic envelopes and boxes can be replaced as the worker proceeds with the shelf reading. Extra bookends should be handy for straightening up shelves.

The Lenin State Library in Moscow has an extensive program for preservation review that is called book inspection. Its purpose is to find maimed books and to do something about them. The book inspector checks every book for dirt, mold, and insects, and also checks the general conditions of very old books. Books that need attention are flagged. Next, the appropriate preservation department collects them from the stacks. Russian librarians are aware of the importance of good stack maintenance and have very stern rules for their stack workers.*

In terms of the stack maintenance work described, opportunities should be provided for staff members to learn more about preservation and minor repairs by attending workshops or, if your library has a preservation department, by working with members of the preservation or conservation departments. There may be an employee, or two, on the staff who will be stimulated or motivated by preservation work. This could lead to the establishment of a minor repairs program (see Figure 4.9) as part of everyday stack work. One cautionary note though: make sure that staff learn the correct repair methods from the experts and use approved supplies in their repairs.

Dust settles mostly on the head of a book. It can be removed with the soft brush attachment of a vacuum cleaner or with a dust cloth. When dusting, hold the book firmly closed with the head angled down so that the dust is not forced down between the pages. Shelves should also be cleaned periodically. Be sure they are completely dry before replacing the books. The collections need an annual vacuuming and dusting.† The annual cleaning program could be instituted during a slower period of library use. You could determine this slow period intuitively or with statistics.

---

*Mangla, P.B. "The Lenin State Library, Moscow." Indian Librarian 24, 4 (1970): 171–173.

†Greenfield, Jane. Books: Their Care and Repair. New York: H.W. Wilson, 1983; p. 21.

Figure 4.9

Stack Section Book Repair Slip	**Stack Section Journal Repair Slip**
Title:	Title/Call #:
Author:	Vol. # Yr. Copy #
Call #:	
Torn pages:	Torn pages:
Pages missing:	Pages missing:
Cover torn:	Cover torn:
Cover off:	Cover off:
Security:	Security:
Call # not readable:	Title not readable:
Defacement:	Defacement:
Attention/other:	
Name _____	Name _____
Date _____	Date _____
Please date and return this slip to the stack office when repairs are completed.	Please date and return this slip to the stack office when repairs are completed.

Stack staff should be encouraged to straighten up shelves (see Figure 4.10) and pull out misshelved materials as a part of their normal routine of shelving, retrieving, and shelf-reading.

Careful upkeep of the stacks also encourages patrons to be neat. In many situations, patrons may be unaware of the correct ways to handle materials. A handout (see Figure 4.11) for patrons with tips may prove beneficial.

Figure 4.10
Stack Section
Stack Problem

Area Assigned _____/_____

| | | | | | | Out |
| Title/Call # | Tight fit | Stuck ins | Bookend | Labels | Boxes | of order |

Name _____ Date _____
Starting time _____a.m._____p.m._____
Finishing time _____a.m._____p.m._____

Figure 4.11
Care and Handling of Bound Library Materials
We Need Your Help

It is important that we offer you some tips on the proper care and handling of library materials.

*   Do not lay a book face down to mark your place. Use a bookmark.
*   Do not eat or drink when handling materials. The crumbs and food wrappers may attract insects or rodents.
*   Do not use post-it notes on books. Also do not use paper clips to mark your place. Remove papers, letters, notes, etc. before returning materials.
*   Do not force a book to open flat when photocopying.

The Physical Environment

Stack staff can be trained to be aware of potential physical problems in their area of responsibility. For example, are any water pipes passing through or near the stack area? Are any windows likely to leak during rainstorms? The stack staff can keep an eye on these pipes and windows. The staff should know where the fire extinguishers and pull boxes are located. Each member of the staff should know what disaster plans exist for the library and what his or her role is in the event of a disaster.

The stack staff can take an active part in environmental control and stack lighting. They can make sure that their stack areas are cleaned frequently. If hygrothermographs are available for stack areas, the staff can monitor them and report adverse humidity conditions. In addition to reporting relamping needs, staff can make sure unnecessary lights are kept off.

The physical environment can overshadow all of your maintenance efforts. The facilities management chapter discusses this topic in greater length.

The Need for Planning

With technological demands, staffing issues, and environmental concerns, the need for planning is imperative.

At any given time, a problem may arise in which all you may be able to do is survive; however it is extremely important to be prepared as much as possible for emergencies by planning ahead and knowing your physical environment. If a flood occurs, threatened materials must be shifted quickly, while accessibility to it by staff and patrons is maintained. Equipment and supplies for fighting floods must be handy to everyone. The supplies must be inventoried regularly because you never want to be without any one item. What do the next six months look like for the library and the stacks? You can never be too prepared. Keep asking yourself, What if...?

Let us consider how to plan. First of all, select your goals, then establish the objectives. Once the objectives are decided, steps are set up for achieving them in an orderly manner. Throughout this planning process remember to consider the feasibility of your goals and objectives. At any given time, every librarian faces options, all of which compete for time and resources. When resources are limited, you must strike a balance between goals and needs.

In addition to short term planning, you must also map out the future. What do you see as likely—and what would you like to see—in library services in two to five years? By compiling statistics now, with the help of a computer, planning for stack growth may become a less stressful responsibility. It is hard to predict what impact technology will have on the stacks. Such information generally takes longer to appear in the library literature; therefore one way to keep informed of possible trends is by browsing technology and business journals.

Strategic management or planning is essential. The concept is relatively new to libraries but has been a theme in the business world since mid-century. Strategic planning deals with the futurity of current decisions, looks at chains of cause and effect, and at the consequences of decisions. It is a process that begins with the setting of organizational aims and develops detailed plans to make sure that the strategies are implemented. This planning necessitates dedication. It is an intellectual exercise with a prescribed set of processes, procedures, structures, or techniques. You must believe it is worthwhile.* Eventually you must act on the plan.

A manager should not undertake the planning process alone. You must include others because eventually you will need everyone's support.

Brainstorming

Brainstorming the possibilities can be fun and rewarding. Just let your imagination go and remember to include your staff in the brainstorming sessions. Brainstorming and innovation go hand in hand. Communication means a free flow of ideas among everyone. If you do not have much experience with groups, it may take a few sessions before the sessions click.

*Steiner, George A. Strategic Planning. *New York: Free Press, 1979; pp. 13–16.*

Once your group is assembled, explain clearly the purpose of the brainstorming session. You should remind everyone that no idea is stupid or to be judged, and everyone is to speak and say whatever comes to mind, and that time is not a factor. All of the suggested ideas must be recorded, perhaps on a flip-chart.

At the conclusion of the session, everyone can then evaluate the ideas. After evaluation, choose one or two of the best ideas. Depending on the goal of the session, you may implement or recommend to the administration the selected ideas.

Rosabeth Kanter's *The Change Masters* offers the following ten rules for *stifling* innovation!*

1. Regard any new idea from below with suspicion—because it's new, and because it's from below.
2. Insist that people who need your approval to act first go through several other levels of management to get their signatures.
3. Ask departments or individuals to challenge and criticize each other's proposals.
4. Express your criticisms freely and withhold your praise.
5. Treat identification of problems as signs of failure, to discourage people from letting you know when something in their area isn't working.
6. Control everything carefully. Make sure people count anything that can be counted frequently.
7. Make decisions to reorganize or change policies in secret, and spring them on people unexpectedly.
8. Make sure that requests for information are fully justified, and make sure that it is not given out to managers freely.
9. Assign to lower-level managers, in the name of delegation and participation, responsibility for figuring out how to cut back, lay off, move people around, or otherwise implement threatening decisions you have made. And get them to do it quickly.
10. And above all, never forget that you, the higher-ups, already know everything important about the business.

Now take these ten rules and do the opposite; thereby laying

*Kanter, Rosabeth Moss. The Change Masters: Innovations for Productivity in the American Corporation. *New York: Simon and Schuster, 1983; p. 101.*

the groundwork to motivate staff to produce creative ideas. If possible, include other library department staff members in the brainstorming sessions. Right now, I bet you are thinking, I don't have time for this. It would not be appropriate to have a discussion of planning without dealing with one of the things that needs the most planning—your time.

Time Management

The head of access services typically faces many interruptions in the course of a day. Some days you may feel at the beck and call of anyone who walks in your door or uses the telephone. But allowing others to constantly control your time is the way to accomplish little work. What you want is an open door policy which means being accessible to those who really need you. Here are some steps to take:

Close the door occasionally.

Establish a quiet hour when you will not be disturbed.

Schedule regular times to be available.

Check the level at which you are delegating. If you fail to delegate, then you end up doing things that others could and should be doing. You may not feel it's necessary to delegate and you can do it quicker—but in the long run that attitude will destroy you.

Should you train more specifically, and give more authority? Are staff bringing decisions and problems to you prematurely without investigating first?

Prepare tomorrow's schedule before you get to the library in the morning. Do not run the risk of beginning your day by reacting to whatever is there before you have considered what is really important.

Start on projects earlier than usual. Allow yourself more time to do it right in the first place and you'll spend less time having to do it over. Do not ignore deadlines. Include some time for yourself every day.

One time management philosophy simply states: If your boss asks you to, do it; if you want to do it, do it; if you can delegate the task, then delegate; or put task away for a few days and if you hear nothing more relax. Not the best but...

Another strategy stresses that you must first decide to manage your time and then arrange each day's tasks in order of priority—the most important tasks are done right away, while the less important tasks are dealt with later. In this way your time is used more effectively.

When you manage time, your job as manager and librarian will become easier.

Monitoring the Stacks

Traditionally, "control" denotes a tight hold by management and projects a negative impression. People shy away from the confrontation and conflict that control signifies. Managers are no different. Librarians view themselves as fair minded people; *control,* however, does not have to be a negative responsibility. The materials must be ordered and returned accurately to the shelves. Control mechanisms come in many forms besides someone just waiting to catch a mistake. An effective training program is one way to standardize the maintenance of stacks. Work leaders and supervisors, armed with problem reports, can monitor the stacks to discover and write-up problems. Feedback from patrons and staff can also assist in the control task. The chapter on staff goes into more details on performance appraisals and other control methods.

As you realize by now, stack management depends on humans not machines. It is labor intensive.

Leading

Does an acceptable substitute for shelvers exist? Could robots replace human shelvers? There have been no serious attempt at using robots as shelvers. Let's just say no stack jobs are yet in jeopardy. Would it ever be worth the effort, especially for those libraries with open stacks? Even mechanized stacks, conveyer belts, or compact shelving break down and staff must retrieve materials.

Stack management may absorb the major portion of your workday but in many ways it is the most consequential role of access services and for the library. All of the activities for proper stack management mentioned add up to a long list of responsibilities for you and duties for the stack staff. It may be necessary to expand job descriptions for the staff. The additional duties can be considered a way of creating variety in a job and making it more interesting and challenging.

Giving the staff a sense of how important all these tasks are to the well-being of the library's collections, and training them to have a feeling of confidence, will yield rich dividends in improved staff morale and productivity. When it comes to the stacks, humans are the most valuable resource.

To sum up this chapter: good stack management is imperative to the proper functioning of a library. Without well maintained stacks the library cannot begin to provide excellent service to its patrons.

5
The Staff

The 15 Year Employee

When Marge started her position, she inherited a long time counterproductive employee, Tony. Keeping Tony working soon became a full time job for Marge. This happens to be a collective bargaining position, with strict guidelines for any personnel actions. Marge is at her wit's end. After analyzing the labor contract and consulting with her supervisor and the personnel department, she decides to terminate Tony's employment. To be done ethically and legally, Marge documents Tony's poor performance and all corrective actions. During the process, Marge encourages Tony to find another job and improve his performance. A discharge case is best supported by proper and complete documentation of the disciplinary circumstances, file building, fair and consistent treatment, and following the concept of corrective disciplinary action. The stronger and more convincing Marge's position, the better her ability to sustain her case or to negotiate a settlement that will serve her purpose.

While undertaking this process, Marge decides to do performance appraisals with each of her staff. Before the individual meetings, she gives questions to each staff member. (See Figure 5.1.)

During the sessions, Marge learns of student workers' not performing their assigned tasks. Staff finds full book trucks

Figure 5.1
Performance Appraisal Questions

1. What accomplishments during the past year are you especially proud of?
2. What do you want to accomplish in the next few months?
3. What skills/activities do you want to learn/do?
4. What at your job do you do well?
5. What at your job could you improve on?
6. What can I as a supervisor do to help you accomplish these goals?

SUPERVISOR'S REMARKS

1. I see these additional areas where you did well.
2. I see these areas in need of improvement.
3. Comments on attendance, job performance, sense of responsibility, initiative, and follow through.

We will talk again after 6 months.

---

hidden throughout the stacks. The resentment is increasing among the staff toward the students. Sometimes Marge could just scream.

Introduction

This chapter examines management of access service staff, the most important resource of any library. Many libraries have one librarian, which creates the need for fully trained and capable staff. Often small libraries and school libraries are one-person operations, with service to students, professionals, and teachers, but with no regular staff. Even in larger libraries, staff, usually not librarians, work the evenings and weekends.

A wide variety of names have been given for these staff positions, including support staff, nonprofessional, paraprofessional, library assistant, paralibrarian, library technician, clerk, or library aid.

Unfortunately, most of these terms have negative connotations.

When staff are supervised, trained, and included in decision making, problems can be resolved, and the solutions are more likely to be fresh, creative, and innovative. Staff must work as a team, with equal sharing of the work. In some libraries, access services staff operate in varying shifts and it may be difficult to build the concept of one team.

Recent library literature has been inundated with controversy regarding the use of students and the nonprofessional at the reference desk. Interestingly, there hasn't been a similar controversy surrounding the staffing pattern of the nonprofessional at the circulation desk. Access services staff, in addition to their departmental duties, also provide reference service. During weekends, evenings and busy times, patrons approach any available staff with reference and technical services questions.

Professionals at the circulation desk occasionally spark an article or two with differing viewpoints. One side sees the head position as professional work while the other side views it as routine and nonprofessional. The professional viewpoint sees the need for a professional to answer questions and promote the services of the library. This controversy is based on the same reasoning behind the view of circulation as routine and menial work. When these stereotypes are displaced, this controversy will disappear.

Today, with new information demands on libraries, a need for an educated work force is a necessity. As automation takes hold of library functions in more and more libraries, access service staff must become computer literate and adaptable to this changing environment.

Entry level jobs have become sophisticated and for some people the quality of the applicants has decreased. In 1987, the New York Telephone Company advertised 780 positions and 21,000 young people applied. The company administered a 50-minute reading and reasoning test geared to the high school level and only 16 percent of the applicants passed the test. In the next decades, the composition of the American youth cohort will shift toward more poor and minority youth, and this will place considerable pressure upon the entry level training system.*

In this day of seemingly widespread illiteracy, you want to pay close attention to the skill level of applicants. The way in which someone fills out their application, their past school and work experiences, and the interviewing process help you determine how applicants will perform on the job. You may decide to hire someone with limited skills, when you see potential and a willingness to learn.

The Staff

Recruitment begins upon the resignation, transfer, promotion, retirement, dismissal, or death of a staff member, or upon the creation of a new position. At various times, you may need to recruit from various walks of life—high school students, women returning to work, older adults, temporaries, or day laborers. One group, growing in size but still relatively new to the labor force, is composed of persons facing various barriers to employment. This group includes limited English speakers, teenage parents, the physically disabled, offenders, alcoholics, drug addicts, and school dropouts. Many of these people will require a great deal of training and instruction but they cannot be overlooked as possible staff.

Expectations, skill level, language skills, ambitions, willingness to work, acceptance of responsibility, interest in development, and level of commitment differ from person to person. There is great diversity in the work force of today.

Depending on other job opportunities, salaries, and geo-

*Osterman, Paul. "Rethinking the American Training System." Social Policy (Summer 1988): 28.

graphical location it may be difficult to recruit and keep employees. You may have a high turnover rate, especially if the job market is open. The access services' position may be perceived as one way of getting a foot in the door of the organization. Benefits abound for the library when you can keep a well-trained and team oriented staff. You must attempt to do everything possible for staff to gain confidence, feel involved, contribute, and make the job more interesting.

People new to the working world are typically highly motivated and ready to work. You as their first supervisor will set the stage for their development. If you think they will fail, you will communicate those feelings directly or indirectly to them. Try to make staff jobs interesting right from the start. Think of some special project that can be assigned a staff member; something that clearly needs doing and will require real thought and creativity.

Being a Manager

What is a manager? I see the manager as someone who creates a system that enables people to do their respective jobs. You get the work done by being the manager, not by trying to be a friend or by trying to bribe staff into doing what they are paid to do. You cannot demand that the staff respect you. You must work hard and when necessary defend your staff. You are paid to make decisions and act upon them; therefore think through the consequences of a decision.

A manager runs the risk of being disliked or perceived as the enemy. Most people do not want to be disliked by anyone, which is why individuals do not want to be managers. Personnel recruitment, appraisal, motivation, and training are all pleasant staff topics. Writings in the professional literature are usually upbeat and only slightly touch on the negative aspects of personnel issues. If the wrong people are hired or promoted or if a promising staff member runs into problems you must take corrective actions, such as discipline and termination. Sometimes a management position forces you to deal with downbeat topics.

You depend on staff to do the work. You cannot do it by yourself. Sooner or later you must get the jobs done through your allotted staff. At times it may not seem as if you have enough staff or time but it is your job as manager to get the work done with the staff you have. Scheduling staff to cover peak use periods becomes a necessity.

Change for the sake of change is not a productive way to run a department. The quality of the change is important. Managers prepare staff for changes by providing them the opportunity to give feedback. Your goal should be to provide the best possible service to your patrons, which you can only accomplish by continually assessing the quality and quantity of the staff's work.

There is often no clear-cut right or wrong in managing. Advantages and disadvantages exist in every decision. The best decision has the fewest drawbacks for that particular situation. The flexibility of your decision making depends on number of staff, hours of operations, and the work.

Mediating problems among staff members is a very tough aspect of your job. Typically it involves an incident where you were not present and where you hear more than one side to the story. Whom do you believe?

Managing staff will be your most difficult responsibility. Unfortunately, one must consider the unsupervised hours worked by staff as somewhat less productive than directly supervised time.

When you begin in a management position, first make an independent account of each staff member. It will be difficult but you must make your own assessments and not listen to others. Never assume staff members know how to do something well even when they have experience. It could be experience in doing it wrong. Also try not to feel that a job is easy because you find it easy. Unfortunately, you do not know how staff were trained, what their skill levels are, or what expectations have been placed on them, unless you have seen them from their start. In addition to full or part time regular staff, you may manage a variety of other people.

Student Workers

Student employees are students with substantial commitments in addition to their library jobs. Their jobs are not their first concern. When hired, student workers should be told what is expected of them. Periodically, you may need to reinforce their responsibilities and clarify points or uncertainties.

As a supervisor you must stress the importance of their work while also realizing the need for some flexibility to accommodate their needs. You need to set clear and consistent rules.

Student workers fill an important void for evening and weekend. Student workers, parttime, and temporary staff are often employed to meet the cyclic needs of the library. They are also useful in meeting seasonal and special project needs. In academic libraries, fall tends to be a much busier time than summer. It is important to take advantage of the summer to vacuum, dust, or shift collections. Students are usually willing to work more hours in the summer.

Volunteers

The use of volunteers varies by the type of library. School libraries are more apt to have volunteers. Public libraries and, for instance, hospitals may also rely on volunteer help. Very few special and academic libraries have volunteer programs.

Some volunteers can quickly master several tasks and perform them with quiet efficiency, some will require constant retraining, and some will start things they never finish. You must evaluate each volunteer, become aware of her or his best talents and limitations, and direct that volunteer to the area where those talents will be most useful. Problem volunteers such as the social butterfly, the grouch, or the incompetent, can be sources of irritation and must be dealt with sooner rather than later.

Duties usually assigned to volunteers are those which might not be considered absolutely necessary but which would enable the library to provide better service. Volunteers make important contributions.

A common staffing problem in libraries is attracting and keeping pages, or shelvers. As better paying jobs become more plentiful, and companies such as fast food restaurants and grocery and department stores offer much higher wages and incentives like transportation, free food, discounts, and even scholarships, the library may experience a greater shortage of workers.

No matter if a staff member stays for six months or six years, he or she needs thorough and consistent training.

The Job

The job is one thing that can provide staff with the satisfaction they need for motivation. Everyone wants job success, recognition, and advancement. A motivated staff is crucial to an effective public service program. A pay raise may not be as effective after the first couple of paychecks. People always want more money and feel they deserve it. I think that respect and acknowledgment of work well done means more to staff, in the long run, than pay.

Each staff member must earn the right to the responsibilities added to her or his job. Too often, managers do it wrong; responsibility is given before staff has shown a willingness to accept it. Managers hope that added responsibility will motivate staff, but staff may see the action as merely an increase in their work load rather than in their responsibility.

A related pattern is the staff member whose work load increases because they work hard and complete tasks on time and free of error. The manager ends up delegating too much work to that individual. Being aware of this phenomena will help reduce the chance of this unconscious abuse.

Access services tasks are perceived as entry level physical labor positions requiring few if any skills. Access services positions are physically and mentally demanding, and the tasks are never ending. There is always shelving, shelf-reading, projects, and desk work. Dealing with patrons at the circulation desk and in the stacks is a demanding and frustrating part of the job. Patrons often react with emotion rather than with thought, especially when they are under stress brought about by deadline pressures. Where are the books? Why can't I have this? The desk and the stacks can nevertheless be the best places to promote the library.

When materials to be shelved are backlogged, your only solution is more hands. Scheduling and thinking will not help if you do not have enough hands. With the fluctuating use of libraries, shelving and desk staff can assist each other during peak use.

Training

With such a diversity of work force and a shrinking labor pool, you need to develop staff. Instead of hiring someone with a particular skill, you may need to build and develop those skills in your own staff. You want to do more than just train; you need to develop staff and keep them. Training for future positions is staff development, which should be the theme running through your training program.

Everyone learns at a different pace; being sensitive to each person's individual pace is beneficial when training. For some people, an explanation given once will be enough while others will need multiple written and oral instructions. Respecting these individual differences is never a waste of time.

An overlooked purpose of training is the early opportunity it gives to compare the performance and conduct of the new staff member to departmental standards. Typically, a collective bargaining agreement includes a probationary period for new staff. This is an extremely important time for staff and you. During this time, monitor the staff member closely. Documentation requires keeping written records even though you may not expect or plan to use the information.

A manual for all staff is indispensable for every library. In addition, a standardized orientation procedure will ensure that staff receives identical information.

Figure 5.2
Circulation training for an automated system
Second Session: Charge/renew,
discharge, hold, and recall

1. Review of session 1
   Conversion on the fly
   Questions

2. Charge/renew
   - Links between patron and book
   - Beeps
   - No beeps, look at message
   - Charge information added to item record
   - Clear charge screen when finished with patron
   - Renewals
   - Book in hand
   - Book not in hand

3. Discharge
   - Link broken (except for books with fines)
   - Beeps
   - No beeps, look at the message

4. Different situations
   - Pieces of materials
   - Circulation review flag

5. Holds/recalls

6. Creating situations for fines
   - System currently used for fines

7. Patron record
   - Patron groups
   - Patron categories
   - Note field

Goals for the training session: Staff will have an understanding of the basic circulation procedures.

Training should cover the importance of accuracy, of effective communication, of diplomacy, and of common sense. It is essential for the staff to know basic procedures and policies as well as methods of handling unusual problems. (See Figure 5.2 for an example of one training session.)

If staff are trained and confident in their abilities, the unusual situation will not be an obstacle.

Focus on safety and prevention of staff injuries during training. For example, using step stools instead of standing on the shelving should be stressed again and again. Whenever possible demonstrate proper methods of lifting, pushing book trucks, clearing photocopier jams, and sitting at a terminal.

You must hold staff accountable for their actions. When mistakes are discovered, work with staff immediately to correct the errors. The first thing to ask yourself is, "How good was their training?" One mistake may mean the loss of a book.

Here is one training strategy. You explain what to do. Then you do it correctly, making sure they see each step of the procedure. Next time, they explain what to do and you do it correctly. Finally, they explain what to do but now you let them do it. You may have them do it a few times. Eventually add "why" to the procedure. You must follow up on how well the training succeeded. Monitor staff performance, check error rates, and examine output throughout training and then at regular intervals.

You can determine who is not working properly also by scheduling and assigning work areas. Assignment of specific work areas encourages a sense of responsibility. If you have no way of discovering who is making the mistakes, the mistakes will keep occurring. People tend to protect one another from criticism. A memo and discussion with all staff may be necessary to correct errors. If one person is performing the task incorrectly, there are probably others doing it wrong as well. Never hope the problem will disappear, confront it head on!

Here is a group exercise in developing work standards: Divide the staff into desk and stack staff. Have each group pick a job that is common to all of its members. Each group should analyze the job until they have it broken down into individual operations and then set a standard for each of the operations. The standard should tell how, or how often in a period of time, the job is to be done. Measurable and observable standards are necessary for objective monitoring of work.

Encourage questions during training. For someone to ask a question, a certain level of knowledge and courage are necessary. Staff should never guess at answering their library clientele; they should either refer a patron to another area or staff member, or arrange for someone to follow up with the patron.

At the conclusion of the formalized training program, you may decide to use the buddy system, pairing new staff with experienced staff members, for a while.

Training and learning are ongoing processes; over time, policies and procedures change. Refresher classes, memos, reminders, and congratulations should be regular parts of the training or development process.

Having a well-trained, efficient and friendly staff performing clear and reasonable policies is the key to contributing excellent service.

Relationship to the Library

Because the staff represent the library to patrons they need to be well informed of other departmental responsibilities. Once staff are comfortable with their required duties, cross-train them in other areas of the library. Each person on the library staff should be given an opportunity to get a picture of the workings of the access services department. Reference, searching, or technical services are usually not available all the hours the library is open. Access services staff hear complaints and questions directed toward other departments. The arrangement for a regular interchange of staff between departments may be one method of achieving a sense of the team.

At 8:30 p.m. Friday, with library closing only half an hour away, staff must be polite and provide the same level of service as if it is 1 p.m. Some patrons can only come to the library late but still they expect all services to be provided. Patrons expect and should expect the best service possible at all times.

Treat the patron the way that you want to be treated. A brief mention of a recurring problem, or a patron complaint, at a staff meeting may make you realize what areas need additional training. We all hope to have a department where staff rush to help patrons and each other with problems, support one another in situations and voluntarily assist each other with work.

The entire staff should be encouraged to make recommendations. Give credit where it is due; recognition is important to everyone.

One quick aside: if at all possible stack workers should have their own private work area with plenty of space. Circulation desk staff usually have their own private work space, as do the staff of every other department. Access to private space allows staff freedom to chat without people (staff and patrons alike) assuming they never work. Just think how often staff with private space stop and chat, especially first thing in the morning. Stack work is tough yet the stereotype of laziness exists because stack staff frequently have nowhere to relax.

Listening

Listening, by everyone, is crucial for achieving satisfaction. Lack of listening causes barriers, alienation, conflict, decreased productivity, miscommunication, resolution of the wrong problems, and loss of good ideas. What can be done? First, eliminate any physical barriers to effective listening. Examine your physical and psychological preparedness, and consider your intent and the potential outcomes from any encounters.

It is extremely important that you listen to staff who are at the front lines. When you are talking with the staff, be it in training, during a performance evaluation or at a meeting, never answer the phone or talk to another person. Devote your full attention to the present conversation. Staff opinions assist in obtaining a clearer insight into what is really happening.

Paraphrasing allows you to check the understanding of a question or idea. When you paraphrase, focus on the content of the speaker's exact meaning. The purpose is to give the speaker a chance to see that you truly heard and understood what they said and to clarify any points.

When you capture and reflect emotion behind the speaker's words, you indicate a caring attitude and an empathy for the speaker. Effectively reflecting the feelings behind an interaction can be a very powerful listening tool. Open-ended questions encourage you and the speaker to clarify meaning.

Before you agree or disagree with a remark you should make certain that what you are responding to is really the message the other party is sending. Miscommunication is the reason behind many problems. When something is said that really bothers you, it may be necessary to talk about it. Hidden agendas or misunderstandings left unaddressed can fester.

Sounds interesting but...

Haven't I heard that before?

When will he get to the point?

These thoughts stifle listening and communication. All of us have a few pet killer phrases that cause us to stop listening. You must actively work towards creating an atmosphere that welcomes listening. Communicating is essential. More time, opportunities, money and relationships are lost through careless, inaccurate listening than through any other activity. This condition will persist until everyone learns to listen and gives it the attention it deserves.

Nonverbal

Nonverbal communication also must be addressed. In libraries, especially with patron interactions so short, nonverbal communication has a significant impact. Avoid crossed arms, frowning, finger tapping, and reading books or newspapers while at the circulation desk. Keep your head up and personal conversations brief. At the circulation desk, staff should be made aware of those actions which create barriers. Staff should be aware of head nodding, eye contact and posture. If your library has an international clientele, cultural differences are factors in daily interactions. Just for instance, for some people standing very close is acceptable behavior, while for others one keeps one's distance. Public libraries require staff to communicate and work with a diverse public.

In a sense, telephone work is the exact opposite of nonverbal communication. All you have is your voice. Answering in a calm clear manner, speaking distinctly, and using a pleasant, courteous and enthusiastic tone of voice is the proper way to communicate on the phone. Concentrate on removing negative tones and phrases from your speech and give the caller your full attention. Of course, understanding how the phone works mechanically is very important, such as putting someone on hold or transferring a call. Use of the word "goodbye" or other definite closing will make it clear that you are finished and intend to hang up the phone.

I have found telephone work to be difficult for some staff who are not native English speakers. On the phone, people speak quickly and often the communication is unclear because of a bad connection. You may need to work with staff on listening and paraphrasing skills.

Complaints may be heard daily. The complaints may be justified. Staff must have guidance when handling troubling situations. Access services is in the position of hearing many complaints and few, if any, compliments. Staff must know why policies and procedures exist because they will need to explain them to patrons. Listening to complaints is stressful and difficult enough even when one is able to articulate a policy in response.

Meetings

It has been calculated that 11 million meetings take place every day in the United States.* Why? A meeting is very often

*Antony, Jay. "*How to Run a Meeting.*" Harvard Business Review 54, 2 (1976): 46.

the only occasion where the staff actually exists and works as a group, the only time when the supervisor or manager is actually perceived as the leader of the team, rather than the boss to whom individuals report. It may also be the only time when the leader is ever perceived to be guiding a team rather than doing a job.*

First, decide on what the meeting is trying to accomplish. Whenever you hold a meeting use an agenda and stick to it. The agenda should not be vague but should define each item on the list. For example, instead of listing "Item 5. Budget," make it "Item 5. Possible ways to reallocate resources."

Schedule your meetings and ask staff ahead of time for any agenda items. Do not go into the meeting unprepared, but plan in advance by preparing an agenda. Before the meeting pass out the agenda to the staff. Do not conduct the meeting in a hurry, but set a time limit. The meeting should be held for a reasonable length of time. Start on time and end on time. Everyone knows how hard it is to sit and listen for a long period. You may decide to schedule important topics at the beginning because the early part of a meeting tends to be more lively and creative.

During meetings, be an effective listener, concentrate on the message, and ask for clarification, when necessary. Let your body support your mind, keep an open mind, and stay focused. Hidden agendas are objectives that people bring to meetings that differ from the planned agenda. Be prepared but not alarmed.

At meetings resist irrelevant interruptions or temptations to go off the track. If at all possible, stay on course. You must remain in control of the meeting. Never single out a staff member for disciplinary action during meetings; instead, talk with them privately. If you have a problem that involves more than one person, a meeting may be the place for discussion.

When conflict is expressed do not stop it, at least staff is giving their opinions. Staff is committing themselves. As long as it is productive, let it happen but when necessary you must stop it. One technique is to gradually shift into another topic.

*Antony, Jay, p. 45.

One way to keep staff involved and participating in the meetings is to have them volunteer to give presentations. For example, have your searcher explain the procedures for locating missing materials.

Even if you have only a few staff members, meet with them regularly. Remember meetings that you have attended: Now, what made one meeting meaningful while another meeting was a waste of time? You may want to ask: Is the meeting held at the proper time? In the proper place? How could meetings be improved? Will minutes be kept? Temperature of the room?

Performance Appraisal

On the other end of the continuum from the meeting is the performance appraisal. Such private meetings with employees are very important, but it may be difficult to convey your judgment in a constructive or painless manner. The sessions should hold no surprises. All conversations should be in private. Evaluation is an ongoing, daily process and not something which is only done at the conclusion of employment. Remember to keep staff informed on how well they are doing or what they need to improve on.

Set goals and objections, and map out how to accomplish them with a set time schedule. When you meet, allow no interruptions, and set aside enough time. You want to achieve a supportive rather than a defensive climate. Listen for ideas, and concentrate your attention on the speaker. Avoid passing judgment, jumping to conclusions, or doing scale type evaluations. Let the evaluation be a set of questions. Give the person notice of when you will meet.

Make your criticism constructive: Get to the point. Present the facts, mention the frequency of occurrence of undesirable actions, and include specific examples. Remember to listen. Seek agreement on the reasons for the problems. Consider organizational factors, lack of knowledge or experience, and personal problems. Engage in problem-solving; agree on a solution and a means to monitor and assess progress; focus on the areas for improvement.

The talk should be based on the goals set previously between you and the staff member. Feedback should be given as close to the time of the event as possible. You must be open to receiving feedback.

The more difficult part of any session is giving negative feedback. Checking for understanding, describing recent examples, being direct, looking at the actions and behaviors and not at the personality, focusing on the effects, identifying the change and results you expect, and problem solving with an attitude of mutuality helps to take away the emotional element.

Labor Relations

Union representation of library employees tends to be uniformly viewed with dismay by academic and public library managers who have and have not experienced it. Employees may be governed by a civil service system (city, state, or federal). You yourself may be in a union.

Your staff may be unionized and covered by collective bargaining agreements but that does not necessarily mean tension needs to exist. If you use tact in dealing with staff, let staff participate in decision making, and communicate effectively, you will eliminate many problems. Be aware of the labor contract and be well trained in the application of personnel policies. Establishment of a friendly, cooperative working relationship with the union steward will likely lead to fewer conflicts. If you perceive the steward as undermining your authority, your relationship may lead to frequent grievances. You will experience few grievances if you demonstrate a genuine concern for employee welfare. There is nothing wrong with working together for the betterment of the library. Sometimes, no matter how hard you try to avoid confrontations, they will occur.

Grievance

When a grievance is filed, you must gain a clear picture of the employee's perception of the problem. Information should be gathered from other sources to ensure that the grievant's perception is not biased or inaccurate. Rumors and lies will fly but you must do everything to get to the truth. After gathering relevant facts, you must make a decision, which must be objective as well as consistent. As a manager you must strive to maintain consistency in whatever you do.

The key to success is early intervention. If disciplinary procedures are correctly applied, if supervisors are sensitive to the needs and concerns of their staff and are cognizant of and properly observe contract requirements, then few grievances are unsolvable.

Discipline

The most difficult duty of a manager is discipline. Discipline is stressful and difficult. Discipline is unpleasant and it is certainly something neither you nor the staff look forward to. Discipline keeps the staff member from repeating the poor act and it tends to keep others from committing the same act. Do not delay discipline and never hold grudges. Disciplinary decisions require fairness, integrity, and objectivity.

Most disciplinary matters involve a two-fold inquiry: first, whether there was just cause for discipline, and second, whether the penalty is appropriate.

When a rule has been broken for the first time by a staff member, talk to the person to ensure that he/she understands the rule in question and what behavior is expected. Avoid emotionalism; do not get into a "yes you did, no I didn't" discussion. If you are angry, it is better to postpone the talk until you cool off.

If the oral warning does not correct the situation, the next step is a written warning. The warning should clearly state that an oral warning was given, what is expected and the next step if a change does not take place. Should the behavior continue, suspension is next. Finally, if there is still no change the staff member can be discharged. When behavior is corrected or improved, provide staff with a clean record, which shows that poor performance was corrected.

The marginal employee who demonstrates an inability to perform consistently within expectations requires personnel action. Inadequate performance may result from any number of factors including technical incompetence, behavioral or physical problems, or inappropriate conduct at work. A common pattern in marginal employees is for performance to improve temporarily after a counseling session, and then to decline until the next session.[*]

The salvaging of a staff member means taking rehabilitative steps and other planned corrective actions, short of termination, so that the investment in recruitment and training is not lost. Considering the employee's performance record, along with the realities of the labor market, ask yourself, has the staff member been adequately trained and supervised.[†] It is difficult to deal with the marginal employee. Unfortunately, I have no clear answer and I have yet to read of the perfect solution.

The discharge of a staff member is viewed as capital punishment by an arbitrator. Match the punishment to the crime. You must follow the termination procedure stated in the contract or personnel manual exactly. Discharges will almost always go to arbitration. Why was this person discharged?

Arbitration

Arbitration is the final grievance step in labor agreements. Your first concern is to try to find a resolution to the problem that gave rise to the grievance. Most organizations seek to avoid

---

[*]*Hafner, Arthur W., and Kibble-Smith, Brian G. "Managerial Responsibility for Employee Discipline."* Library Journal *113, 8 (1988): 41.*

[†]*Hafner, Arthur W., p. 43.*

the uncertainties associated with an arbitration case. Your organization must assist you in making sure that the case is sound and that the evidence supports your position.

Arbitration puts matters in the hands of a neutral third party. Their decision is binding. The decision whether to go to arbitration can only be made after judicious and thoughtful consideration of all factors on a case-by-case basis. Unions and management both often prefer not to use an arbitrator, because of the impact on contract, rights, organization, and policies.

The reality, though, is that early settlements promote good employee relations. You must work closely with others to find solutions to employee relations issue.

Professional Growth

Marge wakes up in the middle of the night. Luckily, she does not remember all the details of the dream.... She had gone to library school with the intention of creating a good working environment for staff and herself, in a place where patrons obtain excellent service. She tries to be fair to staff and give the best service possible to patrons. Lately, however, much of her time is spent on the phone with photocopy equipment companies, shelving books, hearing complaints, protecting staff from unjust criticisms, and recruiting staff. A vision crosses her mind of serenity. "Could it ever happen here?" she wonders.

Don't forget your own professional growth. What can you do to rejuvenate yourself? Burnout comes from frustration. You may be headed for burnout if you need more hours to do less, you cannot sleep, you start forgetting appointments and losing possessions, and you feel more and more irritable, cynical, or disenchanted. Look to rewarding activities outside the library.

Access services is a difficult department to manage, especially when you consider all of the supervisory responsibilities. Supervising is a tough job even in the best of circumstances.

Look at what you may face: a mixture of staff—some care, others don't, there's a high turnover rate and feelings of being underpaid; some won't work hard but others are fast and smart; everyone feels pressure to return materials to the shelves within a short time; there are frictions over staffing the circulation desk for the long hours, including holidays, evenings, and weekends. And of course at all times everyone must be polite to patrons.

Sometimes no matter how hard you try, a backlog of work never goes away; patrons will never fully understand or be satisfied. You can only do so much.

Join associations, get on committees, and get involved in the profession and your library. If not interested in professional involvement at the national level, how about at the state or local level? Look to your own institution for any resources, workshops, or counseling. You will have many annoyances in your job, and you need something to offset or compensate for your work life. You never want to fall into the "Why me?" trap.

6
Facilities Management

The Bat

After lunch, Marge notices a message from reference; a patron complained of a bat in the second floor stacks. The bat is swooping and frightening patrons. Luckily, Marge opens the windows in the stacks and the bat flies out.

When she returns to her office, she finds a note about a stuck elevator. "What do they think I am?" she thinks.

Access services tends to be the liaison between the library and facilities management. Planning, directing, and coordinating the library's physical surroundings with the physical plant department, mail service, housekeeping, and equipment maintenance come under the heading of facilities management.

Since access services staff work throughout the library and staffs the library more hours than other departments, the staff are identified with the library's physical environment.

The access services department has a vested interest in the lighting, booklifts and elevators, heating and cooling, and cleanliness of the library. Developing a good working relationship with facilities personnel and outside repair people is beneficial in a number of situations. For example, when a flood strikes, you know whom to call for fast help. When an elevator breaks down, stack staff may be unable to shelve materials until the elevator is operating.

Some crises are caused by events not under your control. Machines break down, weather is unpredictable, people make mistakes, or information is distorted or delayed. Never expect the job to be free of crises. You must learn to live with these problems and stop worrying about them. You simply can neither anticipate nor control everything. When planning, build in flexibility for those unexpected events. Alternatives give you choices, so that when disaster strikes you will be prepared, as much as possible.

If a "unique" crisis occurs, turn it into an opportunity to try new ideas, develop new procedures, or find more efficient ways to do tasks. A crisis may just be the thing that triggers change you have considered but never instituted. The physical environment of the library supplies its share of crises.

Environmental Control

Environmental control in a library is different from that in many other buildings because it requires air conditioning and air quality control for both people and contents. Library materials last longer when the temperature and humidity remain within a certain range. Heat makes printed matter and other materials brittle. Books must be kept away from radiators. When books are stored in cold places, condensation will form when they are moved to warmer areas.* The temperature should range between 68 and 74 degrees Fahrenheit.

If the air is too moist, mildew forms on books; if it is too dry, materials crack and dry out. The humidity range should be below 70 percent and above 40 percent. To keep humidity in this range you may need to install air conditioning, or use dehumidifiers and fans in the summer; humidifiers or pans of water in the winter. Wide swings in relative humidity are undesirable. Steady conditions, even though not in the optimum humidity range for the contents, are preferable to variations in humidity.

*Greenfield, Jane, p. 20.

Some rare materials may pose especially stringent environmental requirements. Library facilities may segregate the parts of the library that need special care. Note where there is a need for humidity, air cleaning, or other environmental controls.

Environmental control of nonprint materials must also remain as constant as possible. You must take care in deciding where to display and store the collections.

Likewise, equipment such as photocopiers and computers, have special temperature and humidity requirements. Vendors can best detail the environmental requirements of their equipment.

With regard to computers, a major fluctuation in temperature or power may result in a disk crash, permanently damaging the hard disk. Another hazard to the disk occurs when any liquid comes in contact with the disk surface.

Photocopiers need to be in a cool, nonhumid, ventilated area to prevent paper jamming and other problems. To put paper in the copier properly, check the arrow on the paper wrapping. Never leave opened packages of paper; place all of the paper in the photocopiers. Paper exposed to the elements cause frequent jamming of the copiers. Also, opened packages of paper invite theft.

Staff and patrons are also affected by the library's environment. Access services staff hear patrons' complaints of being too hot or too cold in the library. Staff cannot work effectively when sweat is streaming down their faces.

Air quality is another area of concern—the "sick building" syndrome is receiving a lot of attention in the periodical literature. Photocopiers and other equipment produce ozone and other pollutants and also stir up dust. This may affect materials and people. An air handling system is necessary to control the quality of the air.

Few aspects of library buildings are more important than lighting. Light causes fading and other chemical deterioration of books. The spectrum of least to most damaging lighting is: incandescent, fluorescent, daylight, and direct sunlight.

Turning off lights when not in use, installing ultraviolet sleeves on fluorescent light bulbs, and installing ultraviolet filters or curtains over windows and skylights are steps to lessen light damage.* Incandescent lights should never be put in exhibition cases.

Lighting is in the stacks, offices, hallways, stairwells, and study areas. Not only does lighting affect materials and people but lights require maintenance. The replacement of bulbs and tubes is a never ending job.

Staff and patrons feel more secure with plenty of lights, especially outside the building, or in areas of the building without windows. No one likes to be in a dark area alone.

Keys

Who controls keys, distributes them, imposes charges for lost keys, and keeps records of all assigned keys?

Keys should be identified by code or number and should never indicate doors they will open. Store any keys that are not assigned to individuals on a regular basis in a highly secure location. What about access to the building when it is closed? Janitors, custodians and security personnel typically require access in such cases.

A system for controlling and auditing locks and keys minimizes the number of master and building entrance keys that are given out. Restrict access and distribution of master keys to those whose duties require them.

Staff is responsible for maintaining possession of their keys at all times. Obtain a signature from staff when a key is issued. Keys should never be loaned out. Remind staff never to leave keys lying around or in unlocked desks. Keys can be quickly and easily duplicated. If an employee is terminated or assigned to new duties, collect his or her keys. Do this prior to releasing a terminated employee's final pay.

*Greenfield, Jane, p. 20.

Another important issue to decide is whether or not to charge a deposit on keys. Probably there should be no charge for regular staff but students, temporaries, or volunteers should be charged. You must consider who has access to what levels of security, and who has keys to reset alarms or open secured areas, and who holds keys for emergency situations.

Key control is the first line of defense against theft and crime. During training, stress the importance of keys to staff.

Alarms

Keys are related to alarms. You need keys to clear alarms, to engage emergency exit door alarms, and to lock anything up during fire drills.

Alarms notify us that something is wrong. When one door's emergency exit alarm goes off often, you may discover a security problem. This may also indicate a need to look at the signs in the area. Alarms should be treated with concern and not as a source of irritation. An alarm exists for a reason.

Emergency exit doors are fitted with panic bars but even if audibly alarmed, unless staff is in the vicinity, anyone can relatively easily use them undetected.

An alarm or ringing bell at closing lets patrons and staff know the library is closing soon. An alarm may be the only way to attract people's attention. Some libraries announce the library's closing over an intercom system in addition to sounding an alarm.

Fire

Detection Systems

Fire detection systems may detect heat, smoke, or ionization. The fire marshal in your area can advise what is acceptable

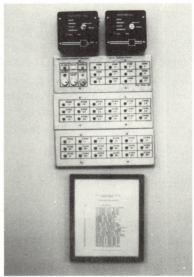

Emergency exit door.   ***Detection systems***
                                     control panel.

for your library. They can also provide you with fire manuals especially written for libraries. Fire detection is something most people do not give a second thought to, but it is the most important security system in the library. It must be taken seriously. Do your research on available systems for your library.

Sprinkler Systems

Fire prevention means no smoking, checking trash cans for cigarette butts, making certain that outsiders (such as workmen and delivery people) do not smoke, policing areas, and checking on library cleanliness. When you prevent fires, sprinkler systems will not be set off. More and more libraries are having sprinkler systems installed.

For some librarians, this policy produces a fear of water damage to their materials but as long as systems are properly installed and tested there should be no cause for concern. The

Sprinkler system.   ***Fire extinguisher.***

potential great benefit of the sprinkler systems outweighs anything else.

Fire Extinguisher

Fire extinguishers must be plentiful, in full view, and inspected on a regular basis. Also, staff should be trained in their use. As expected in this day and age more than one type of extinguisher exists. A pressurized water extinguisher is best for use on paper and wood fires, but is not to be used on electrical equipment or on flammable liquids. Halon 1301 or Halon 1211 extinguishers are appropriate for use on any indoor fire. Dry chemical extinguishers are usable on any fire but leave a powdery residue. The CO_2 extinguisher is suitable for electrical and flammable liquid fires and leaves no residue, but is not as good on wood and paper fires.* The extinguisher itself has been redesigned for easier use.

Staff must be careful whenever using an extinguisher. Staff may not be trained in its use and in an emergency may become flustered and forget where it is located or how to use it. Someone could be harmed. Staff must first call the fire department before ever touching a fire extinguisher.

Fire Drill

First, the alarm goes off, the fire department is notified, and the library is evacuated. Staff may close doors and windows to decrease circulation of air. If you have a cash register, lock it up. Turning off the security system guarantees that no one will be stopped by a locked gate. An extinguisher should only be used after everyone has left the library and the fire department is on the way. You must know your library's procedure for relocating evacuated people. Where should they go? What is staff's responsibility in clearing the library? What about money or cash registers? Who is the last to leave?

Even during a drill, make sure the evacuation is handled like a real emergency. People tend to assume a false alarm but you must clear the library and behave as if the situation were urgent. You just never know when a real fire emergency may occur. Sprinkler systems are installed because people do not leave when alarms sound.

Water Damage

Fighting fires, by sprinklers or firefighters, produces water damage. In addition, water damage may result from breaks in

*Morris, John. The Library Disaster Preparedness Book. *Chicago: ALA, 1986.*

Note overhead pipe: a potential for water damage.

water and steam pipes, construction operations, rainstorms, hurricanes, tornadoes, earthquakes, leaking roofs and windows, and floods. You must be prepared.

There is persistent danger of flooding when pipes are located in the library. If one of the heating/cooling pipes breaks or leaks, the water spreads throughout the area. Watching out for electrical wiring, hazards in the flooded room, and slippery floors lessens the risk of injury to staff.

When a flood does strike, rest and relax for a few minutes before tackling it. Take the time to prepare staff, go over your prepared plan, and get the equipment. Never allow anyone to enter a flooded area until it is certain there is no possibility of electrical hazards.

While the Yale University Medical Library was undergoing the early stages of its recent renovation project, the New Haven area had one week of steady heavy rains. At one point behind one basement wall stood six feet of water and on the other side was library materials. During one daily inspection, a staff member discovered water pouring into the library side through an electrical outlet, which was missing one plug. Luckily, the water pouring in was discovered early but not before water had spread. It does not take very long for water damage to occur.

Here is a water security checklist:

1. Know the water hazards — geographical and man-made.
2. Check automatic sprinklers, pipes, drains, toilets, drinking fountains, and turn-off points.
3. On rainy days have staff inspect the library for any signs of water leaking into the library.
4. Check for low shelving and materials stored on the floor or close to it; nothing should ever be stored actually *on* the floor.
5. Encourage regular maintenance of the facilities.
6. Incorporate an inspection routine in your closing and opening procedures; post phone numbers for emergency calls.
7. Have flood fighting equipment and supplies accessible and in working order.
8. When possible periodically perform a flood drill with staff; depending on where your library materials are located, you may find yourself concerned with the water itself.

The Yale University Medical Library has some off-site storage, called the annex, of older library materials in the subbasement of a medical research building. During one evening trip to collect materials from the annex, a staff member discovered water leaking from a pipe. Staff quickly called me at home. Our physical plant department was then notified. Physical plant personnel informed us that no one was to enter the space until the water was checked for contamination. When I arrived at the annex, a person in protective clothing, mask, and Geiger counter was collecting water samples. About a half hour later the call came in. Luckily, the water was safe and we could get on with fighting the flood and protecting the materials. Apparently, something from a laboratory had clogged the pipe.

Sometimes restrooms can cause water problems. For example, if for some reason the water is turned off, people attempting to use it may leave a faucet turned on; when the water supply is restored, a flood results. If you ever have a water shut-off, make certain that signs are posted and enforced. Plugged toilets can be another water hazard. Surprisingly, it is sometimes plugged intentionally with toilet paper. Some libraries have had to close their restrooms because of constant flooding of the library due to mischief with the toilets.

Windows and skylights are beautiful. Unfortunately, not all are properly engineered and installed. Resulting problems range from glare and heat penetration to leakage.

Housekeeping

If an area has clutter, patrons will add to the mess. The situation will only get worse. Garbage in the stacks encourages patrons to be messy. When the area is clean and there are plenty of wastebaskets, garbage will not pile up. Also debris or clutter from food and drink increases work for cleaning staff. Clutter gets in the way, especially in emergency situations.

Another potential danger for a book collection is damage caused by insects. The stack staff can watch for signs of infestations. If any insects are seen, the stack supervisor should be informed. In addition, animals, birds, and everything else could become unwanted patrons. Everyone should keep their eyes open.

Reasons for having a policy on no food or drink abound: grease from hands and spilled drinks and food may soil materials, attract vermin, and undermine the library's public image.

An exhibit on the effects of food and drink on materials and potential insect problems may raise awareness of the problem and concern for library materials. This gives the patron an opportunity to see the importance of not allowing food or drink in the library.

Spills and food stains cause rapid deterioration of materials, resulting in costs for their replacement (if possible) or repair and preservation. The presence of food and drink also creates an environment that attracts insects and vermin, which damage materials. Even an empty food wrapper will attract vermin. Food may also lead to mold and mildew damage. A clean environment inhibits infestation of materials and the building with vermin and decreases the cost of housekeeping. You may choose a cat for mouse control!

Some libraries fine patrons who are caught eating or drinking in the library. For example, the University of Oklahoma Library issues such citations. The citations are filed with the student affairs office, which handles any appeals and completes the paperwork required to place a fine on the student's university account.[*]

Food or drink must be confiscated. Staff should not eat or drink in public spaces. The food or drink that staff bring into the library should be kept out of public view. Remind staff not to eat in their offices.

Successful implementation depends upon the recognition by all library staff that they share the responsibility for preventing food and drink from coming into the library. Everyone must do their part.

Signs

Here is one sign likely visible in all libraries:
PLEASE — FOOD AND DRINK ARE NOT PERMITTED.

Signs are needed to guide patrons through the stacks and provide information about the library. Directional signs should be unambiguous and easily seen. The lettering must be clear and readable from a distance. The number of signs should be kept to a minimum, for patrons are unlikely to read large numbers of signs. Whenever location of services or materials change, immediately put up signs.

---

[*]*Weaver-Meyers, Pat L., and Ramsey, Stephen D. "Fines for Food: A Citation System to Control Food and Drink Consumption in the Library."* College & Research Library News 51, 6 (1990): 536.

You may have one staff member designated as the official signmaker. There are software programs that produce nice signs and the process is easy and fun. Someone should also check the signs for correct spelling and clarity.

Communication

Where is the phone? Do you supply beepers? Where will new phones be located? Will you provide pay phones or internal phones? An intercom system? Quick contact with staff or patrons is important. In this age of beepers, people are always asking for a phone to answer a call.

Phones located outside the library are necessary for security and safety. Communication lines galore are mandatory today because of computers and facsimile machines. Communication has become more integral to the library facility.

Facilities

Virtually every improvement in library services seems to require more equipment, creating an insatiable appetite for electrical power. Power strips usually lie beneath the floor or in the ceiling. Equipment required for automation and in response to technology makes demands on space, environment, power supply, and communication systems.

With this increased demand for electrical power, old wiring may not be safe. Today, concerns over power drains and surges are being addressed. One can purchase surge protectors or power line conditioners to alleviate surges and drains.

Other Issues

Elevators move materials as well as people. An awareness of the elevator's various buttons and switches, weight limits, and phone come in handy, if you ever become stuck in an elevator.

Also, the knowledge may allow you to know when or if a service call is necessary. A power failure will cause the elevator to stop, no matter who or what is in the elevator. Staff must be instructed on leveling an elevator with the floor. Staff should never lift a book truck off an elevator. Trucks must roll off the elevator without any lifting of the book truck. Book lifts or dumbwaiters carry only materials and never people, but they can also break down and cause work flow interruptions.

Storage areas for forms, shelving, bookends, boxes, supplies, and records need to be secured in clean, dry spaces. Materials should not be left on the floor. An organized storage area makes life easier and safer. No accumulation of clutter should be allowed. Staff should be able to find what they are searching for without any frustration.

Libraries receive packages in all sizes and shapes from all over the world. Shipping and receiving usually occurs at a loading dock. Your department may not be directly responsible for the area but an awareness of the facility may prove useful to you.

Your staff works throughout the library at all hours of the day. During the course of a shift, health and safety issues may arise. What is that chemical odor? What is that oozing? Is that exposed asbestos? Staff may feel threatened. Fortunately, health and safety material sheets exist for most chemical items found in a library. This type of information should be available for staff to consult whenever a question arises.

You may not have direct responsibility for facilities management but access services are affected by it. The physical environment is central to the library, staff, and materials. There is very little in library literature about these topics. I hope this changes quickly.

7
The Future

The access services staff of the future will become more intimately involved in ensuring access to information for every patron. This opportunity to take a leadership role in preparing libraries for the quickening pace of change forces us to have confidence in our abilities and to innovate and experiment. We cannot afford to sit back and wait to be asked. People involved in access services must prepare now for their expanded library role.

Librarians must constantly monitor the outside world for technological trends that may affect libraries. Access services need to be proactive in providing information and services. Do not wait for reference to give you that compact disc or software to circulate.

Circulation is the only service of librarianship that does not have a publication solely devoted to its interests. Circulation services are usually discussed under the rubric of public services. In such cases, concerns about reference or information services overshadow concerns about circulation.

A first step in promoting access services is to establish an access services network. A newsletter should be created targeting access services or circulation librarians from all types of libraries. The publication could act as a clearinghouse for the circulation information world. This allows for the sharing of ideas, policies, procedures, forms, solutions, and problems, while building professional ties.

Becoming active in American Library Association committees is another way to have a voice and representation on the national level.

When circulation librarians leave their position, they must
keep advocating circulation's contribution. Never turn your
back on circulation and never be embarrassed of your roots.

We must hold up our heads and not let circulation be subor-
dinated to other aspects of librarianship. Since access services
have never been defined in a straightforward manner, the duties
involved in administering them vary from library to library. The
head is typically a rookie and the work is not considered
glamorous in the profession. For many reasons, circulation and
access services have not been given the credit they deserve. The
following was written in 1933 and is still true nearly sixty years
later:

> It is the belief of the authors that the work of the loan department
> has received too little emphasis in comparison with the work of
> other departments of the library. The possibilities of the full
> development of book service to readers have not been realized.*

Access services are different from reference or technical services, especially in the nature of the work performed. In access
services you rely heavily on staff and therefore it is highly
management oriented. In your role as a manager in the 1990s,
you may face legal issues in employment practices, such as sex
discrimination, AIDS, use of lie detectors, drug testing, law suits
over the giving of negative references, age discrimination, and
safety and health issues.

Managers of access services often oversee a diverse work
force. In the future, one can expect an even more multicultured
staff. More and more people will be entering the work force that
previously did not work. The manager must have knowledge,
sensitivity, and awareness of this cultural diversity. Staff must be

---

*Brown, Charles H., and Bousfield, H.G. Circulation Work in College and
University Libraries. *Chicago: ALA, 1933; p. viii.*

recognized, valued, and respected for this diversity. You no longer want to melt down the staff. Your difficult task is to manage the diversity to achieve commitment, loyalty, and production. Your first step is to use your listening skills.

Jobs will be changed and redesigned in the future library. I do not doubt that access services jobs will be different but I cannot guess to what extent. The shelving and control of materials will remain basic to the library.

Books and materials will stay. You cannot have a material-less library. Technology will open up library walls, libraries may become resource centers, but materials still need to be organized. Nonprint materials will take a more active part in collections.

Still, for the foreseeable future at least one thing remains true: if materials are not shelved daily, you will hear complaints from patrons. (If you do not have an organized collection, everyone might as well leave.)

Shelving is physically demanding as well as mentally stressful. Loaded book trucks can weigh up to 400 pounds. The daily contact with patrons, often when they are frustrated and angry, produces stress. Access services staff hear complaints but few, if any, compliments. Some patrons treat access services staff as menial laborers. Some patrons even feel that finding a book on the shelf cannot compete (in sophistication) with a compact disk database.

Technology and computers do not shelve books, deliver documents (original materials), or perform interlibrary loan duties. The only solution to many access problems is staff. You need staff and will always need staff. Approach every task as professionally concerned staff providing a high level of service.

You do need staff people who are computer literate, however, and you may need to train your staff in computer skills yourself. Technology has changed the face of circulation control, especially the automated integrated system. Staff have access to more information today than ever before. Technical services are no longer a mystery. Staff know whether a book has been ordered, received, processed, or cataloged. Also, the facsimile machine is changing the shape of interlibrary loan and document delivery. It is impossible to know whether present or future technology will further revolutionize access services.

Even if the term *circulation* is not replaced by *access services*, the contribution to libraries and the profession of this conglomeration of activities and services needs acknowledgment. We must strive to gain the credit due access services.

Graduate library programs must begin including access services responsibilities in their curriculums. The managerial aspects, automated or even manual control systems, the research possibilities of use studies, the historical approach, and the future of access services could easily be incorporated into any library graduate program.

> Publishers and librarians are both engaged in serious long term planning efforts. Both must make major investment decisions among an array of choices, each of which involves considerable financial and professional risk. There is not enough money to do everything or even most things, that technology offers. To the degree academic library and publishing planning efforts can be done conjointly, fewer mistakes will be made and less money wasted.
>
> Researchers will continue to present conference papers and to write journal articles and the occasional book and seek credible publication outlets for these materials. Publishers will remain the principal filterers, financiers and distributors of this type of research information, libraries the primary purchasers and access points: publishers as gatekeepers, libraries as gateways.
>
> We are already technically capable of doing far more than our budgets will ever allow. The basic level of information exchange while improving is likely to remain below state-of-the-art for a long time. Librarians have always known how to do much more than they could afford to do and have made choices accordingly.*

No matter what shape information takes in the future, access services will be there. The future of access services is bright and limitless.

Hunter, Karen. "Academic Librarians and Publishers." Journal of Library Administration 9, 4 (1988): 47.

Annotated Bibliography

Introduction

Childers, Thomas, and Van House, Nancy A. "The Grail of Goodness: The Effective Public Library." *Library Journal* 114, 16 (1989): 44–49.
   In 1988–1989 the authors performed a national study to discover what comprises an effective public library. The study was intended to help define effectiveness and was meant to disclose the broad views people are inclined to take of the public library. Constituents included community leader, local officials, friends, trustees, users, managers, and service librarians. Six top indicators were convenience of hours, range of materials, staff helpfulness, range of services, services suited to the community, and materials quality.

Hunter, Karen. "Academic Librarians and Publishers: Customers versus Producers or Partners in the Planning of Electronic Publishing?" *Journal of Library Administration* 9, 4 (1988): 35–47.
   Advocates that academic libraries and publishing planning efforts be done conjointly: fewer mistakes will be made and less money wasted. Publishers have financial constraints just as libraries do, and the two must talk to each other. The author feels that in the near future the basic roles of academic librarians and publishers will not change. Areas of discussion include new product and service development, CD-ROM, electronic document delivery, future of scholarly book publishing, and networking.

Kilgour, Frederick G. "Toward 100 Percent Availability." *Library Journal* 114, 19 (1989): 50–53.
   Calculates the improvement in availability that a collection of machine-readable books would bring about: immediate access to contents, and no worrying about whether something is in circulation or has been

misshelved. Nonretrieval could still be due to a patron's keying in something incorrectly, however.

McHale, Cecil J. "Professional Duties in the University Library Circulation Department." *Wilson Library Bulletin* 6 (1932): 359–360.
Details professional duties in the university library setting, encourages the thorough training and selecting of student assistants, and discusses bibliographical consultants, measuring the use of books, and inter-departmental ramifications.

Richardson, Selma K., editor. "Children's Services of Public Libraries." Allerton Park Institute, 23. Urbana: University of Illinois Graduate School of Library Science, 1977.
Papers presented at the Allerton Park Institute, November 13–16, 1977. Focused upon the totality that is children's services in public libraries. What are we doing? Why? For whom? How? Comprehensive approach.

Chapter 1

Balkema, John. "Topics in Library Technology: Charging Systems." *Bulletin of the Medical Library Association* 54, 1 (1965): 33–37.
Methods of circulation control, using the Newark Charging System as a prototype, are reviewed; the devices being used are described.

Beaubien, Denise M.; Keese, Erich; Emerton, Bruce; Primack, Alice L.; and Seale, Colleen. "Patron-use Software in Academic Library Collections." *College and Research Library News* 49, 9 (1988): 661–667.
The University of Florida guidelines for purchasing, cataloging, circulating, and preserving software. Raises questions and suggestions for implementation.

Bousfield, Humphrey G. "Circulation Systems." *Library Trends* 3 (Oct. 1954): 164–176.
This discussion of then-current circulation systems in college, university, and public libraries is concerned with saving borrowers' time, reducing costs, speeding processes, and allowing circulation librarians to devote more time on the professional level.

Brown, Charles H., and Bousfield, H.G. *Circulation Work in College and University Libraries.* Chicago: American Library Association, 1933.
Even though written in 1933, still an interesting book on important principles, methods and practices. Broad approach to circulation control. Considered comprehensive work, still consulted and cited today.

Burgin, Robert, and Hansel, Patsy, editors. *Library Overdues: Analysis, Strategies and Solutions to the Problem.* New York: Haworth Press, 1984. (First published in *Library & Archival Security* 6, 2/3 [1984].)
   Collection of articles on the topic of overdues. Includes: More hard facts on overdues, How one public library copes, Novel approaches, Dealing with defaulters?, Overdues and academic libraries, hospital libraries, and school libraries, Library automation, and a bibliography.

Buschman, John; Reilly, Rebecca; and Andrilli, Ene. "Smart Barcoding in a Small Academic Library." *Information Technology and Libraries* 7, 3 (1988): 263–270.
   Describes the smart barcoding project of an entire circulating collection of 160,000 volumes, from initial planning to conclusion. The project took 4 weeks in August.

Cabeceiras, James. *The Multimedia Library.* New York: Academic Press, 1978.
   Contains some useful information about nonprint materials.

Carr, H.J. "Report on Charging Systems." *Library Journal* 14 (May–June 1889): 203–214.
   Librarian at the Grand Rapids, Michigan, Public Library reviews then-current policies on loan periods, renewals, fines, procedures, and privileges, from a survey of 203 libraries.

Damas, Samuel. "Microcomputer Software Collections." *Special Libraries* (Winter 1985): 17–23.
   Overview and early discussion of management of software collections.

Davis, Betty Bartlett. "The Great Barcoding Project: Barcoding 400,000 Volumes in 13 Days at Indiana State University Libraries." *Library Hi Tech* 11 (1985): 67–69.
   In 13 days, 68 staff members, working with volunteers and student assistants, barcoded 400,000 books. Barcode labels—containing location designation, call number, and barcode number—were produced from and linked to the bibliographic database. Recommends not scheduling the event until labels have been received.

Ellison, John William, and Coty, Patricia, editors. *Nonbook Media: Collection Management and User Services.* Chicago: American Library Association, 1987.
   Series of writings on 22 nonbook formats by experts who take the practical approach: definition, history, and characteristics of each medium; selection; maintenance and management including storage and care; other concerns. Circulation policies with comments on fines and loan periods are included.

Epstein, Susan Baerg; Freeman, Gretchen; and Iacono, Pauline. "Custom Barcoding As a Better Way." *Library Journal* 114, 14 (1989): 156–159.
A discussion of how to barcode label your collection without tears. Advocates custom barcode labeling for library systems with many variously sized branch locations. Whether the approach is a few days of blitz by teams or a long term project, smart barcodes offer an alternative to the linking and keying of item records for each item in the collection. Benefits are explained.

Fried, Ava Krinick. "A Reevaluation of Circulation Policies." *Special Libraries* 72, 3 (1981): 284–89.
Studies conducted at a medical school library to evaluate the cost effectiveness of overdue loan procedures and circulation loan period policy led to changes in the loan period.

Gaudet, Jean Ann. "Automating the Circulation Services of a Small Library." *Library Resources and Technical Services* 31, 3 (1987): 249–55.
A discussion of the management problems encountered in very small school libraries. Gives reasons why procedures recommended in the literature may not be applicable for small libraries. Presents procedures for implementing a circulation system in a small school library.

Geer, Helen. *Charging Systems*. Chicago: American Library Association, 1955.
This dated, but historically valuable and impartial overview of charging systems used in public, college, and university libraries was designed as a guide to the selection process.

Gervasi, Anne, and Seibt, Betty Kay. *Handbook for Small, Rural, and Emerging Public Libraries*. Phoenix: Oryx Press, 1988.
A discussion for communities, lay people, and librarians about providing services to areas that are not part of large metropolitan centers and to areas that have not had service before. Starts from scratch— from choosing a director to choosing the furniture. The basics of circulation are briefly discussed.

Getz, Malcolm. "More Benefits of Automation." *College and Research Libraries* 49, 6 (1988): 534–44.
The benefits of an automated library system are described, measured, and valued in dollar terms. Discussion includes automated circulation system as well as an automated catalog and is measured from the patron's point of view.

Intner, Shelia. *Circulation Policy in Academic, Public, and School Libraries*. New York: Greenwood Press, 1987.

This description of current circulation policies based on surveys of academic, public, and school libraries provides useful information.

Jestes, Edward C. "Manual versus Automated Circulation: A Comparison of Operating Costs in a University Library." *Journal of Academic Librarianship* 6, 3 (1980): 144–150.
This study comparing the operating costs of a manual and an automated circulation system showed that direct labor costs were reduced but the computer equipment and maintenance costs more than offset this saving. However, since overall automated circulation costs were projected to increase more slowly than overall manual costs, an increase in activity would equal out the cost differences.

Klerk, Ann de. "Barcoding a Collection—Why, When, and How." *Library Resources & Technical Services* 25 (Jan./Mar., 1981): 81–87.
A full discussion of barcoding.

Lewis, Shirley. "Nonprint Materials in the Small Library." *Library Resources & Technical Services* 29, 2 (1985): 145–50.
Outlines practical steps to take when mainstreaming nonprint materials: selecting, ordering, cataloging, processing, circulating, and shelving materials in a small library.

Linderfelt, K.A. "Charging-Systems." *Library Journal* 7 (June 1882): 178–82.
The librarian of the Milwaukee Public Library discusses charging systems of the day and details questions to be answered when choosing a system. A thorough explanation of Milwaukee's charging system over 100 years ago.

Matthews, Joseph. *Choosing an Automated Library System.* Chicago: American Library Association, 1980.
Intended primarily for use by medium and small libraries. Presents a plan of action to consider, select, and implement an automated system.

Matthews, Joseph, editor. *A Reader on Choosing an Automated Library System.* Chicago: American Library Association, 1983.
A series of reprinted articles pertaining to the consideration, selection, and implementation of automated library systems, intended to complement *Choosing an Automated Library System* (1980). The articles are concerned with identifying needs, the alternatives, tools to use in performing an analysis, the selection process, contracts, the practical side of installation, and training. A little out of date but still contains useful information.

Matthews, Joseph, and Hegarty, Kevin, editors. *Automated Circulation.* Chicago: American Library Association, 1984.
     Proceedings of a preconference sponsored by LAMA in 1982 on automating circulation: 15 chapters on contract negotiations, costs, budgets, implementation, and public relations.

Mosborg, Stella. "Measuring Circulation Desk Activities Using Random Alarm Mechanisms." *College and Research Libraries* 41, 5 (1980): 437–44.
     A survey in 1978 of circulation staff activity at University of Illinois–Urbana, based on random checks of activity during randomly selected days, showed that over half of the staff's time was spent on patron interaction, discharging, filing, and charging or renewing. The activity that accounted for the largest percentage of time was absenteeism, 26.4 percent of student staff time.

Plummer, Mary W. "Loan Systems." *Library Journal* 18 (July 1893): 242–246.
     A discussion of loan systems in 1893.

Scholtz, James C. *Developing and Maintaining Video Collections in Libraries.* Santa Barbara, Calif.: ABC-Clio, 1989.
     This extensive, interesting, and detailed discussion of videos focuses primarily on public libraries but will also appeal to library systems and school libraries. Limited to ½-inch videocassettes, but concepts can be applied to other formats.

Smisek, Thomas. "Circulating Software: A Practical Approach." *Library Journal* 110, 5 (1985): 108–109.
     An account of Minneapolis Public Library's decision to circulate software. Selection criteria were quality, affordability, and popularity; the program was a success.

Thomason, Nevada. *Circulation Systems for School Library Media.* Littleton, Colo.: Libraries Unlimited, 1985.
     Intended to assist school library media specialists in becoming familiar with circulation systems. Practical basics are provided along with samples of policies for media centers.

Upham, Lois N., editor. *Newspapers in the Library: New Approaches to Management and Reference Work.* New York: Haworth Press, 1988.
     Articles on the physical control of newspapers, including preservation issues.

Wall, Thomas B. "Nonprint Materials: A Definition and Some Practical

Considerations on Their Maintenance." *Library Trends* 34, 1 (1985): 129–140.
Good discussion of nonprint materials.

Walton, Robert A., and Bridge, Frank R. "Automated System Marketplace 1990: Focusing on Software Sales and Joint Ventures." *Library Journal* 115, 6 (1990): 55–66.
The activity of automated systems in the 1990 marketplace is discussed and analyzed.

Ward-Callagham, Linda. "The Effect of Emerging Technologies on Children's Library Service." *Library Trends* 36, 1 (1987): 437–447.
Stresses that technology is useful as a tool and is found to deliver what is needed in a practical manner. Microcomputers, databases in online and laser disc formats, video, and cable television are beginning to find applications in children's services. Are children allowed to borrow these materials? This article encourages librarians to be willing to explore possibilities of emerging formats for children.

Weaver-Meyers, Pat; Aldrich, Duncan; and Seal, Robert A. "Circulation Service Desk Operations: Costing and Management Data." *College & Research Libraries* 46, 5 (1985): 418–431.
This example of a cost study for circulation service desk operations using observers is important for those undertaking similar research.

Yagello, Virginia E., and Guthrie, Gerry. "The Effect of Reduced Loan Periods on High Use Items." *College and Research Libraries* 36, 5 (1975): 411–414.
A study of the relationship between book loan periods and use in the Physics Library at Ohio State University showed that reduction of the loan period of high use items to one week increased circulation over a year's time by 20.9 percent. Previously, circulation statistics had declined.

Chapter 2

Association of Research Libraries. *Electronic Mail.* SPEC kit 149. Washington, D.C.: ARL, Nov.–Dec. 1988.
Details use of electronic mail.

Association of Research Libraries. *Photocopy Service in ARL Libraries.* SPEC kit 115. Washington, D.C.: ARL, June 1985.
Summary of 79 survey responses on descriptions of services, price lists, position descriptions, advertisements, user surveys, contracts, legal issues.

Bell, Jo Ann, and Speer, Susan. "Bibliographic Verification." *College and Research Libraries* 49, 6 (1988): 494–500.

Questions whether the lending library really needs a complete bibliographic citation to supply the requested item, and suggests that individual libraries reach mutual agreement before modifying the verification procedure.

Boucher, Virginia. *Interlibrary Loan Practices Handbook.* Chicago: American Library Association, 1984.

A practical work—keep it in the ILL office.

Brown, Steven Allan. "Telefacsimile in Libraries." *Library Trends* 37, 3 (1989): 343–356.

Discusses the library applications (document delivery, reference, speed, cost, user satisfaction, impact on library's operation), and recent technological developments of facsimile. Raises issues about cost and suggests what questions to ask when comparing systems.

Dutcher, Gale A. "DOCLINE: A National Automated Interlibrary Loan Request Routing and Referral System." *Information Technology and Libraries* 8, 4 (1989): 359–370.

A detailed and very informative discussion of DOCLINE: background and a nice overview.

Jackson, Mary. "Facsimile Transmission: The Next Generation of Document Delivery." *Wilson Library Bulletin* 62, 9 (1988): 37–43.

A detailed discussion of facsimile machines. The technology has changed since this article was written, but the questions it raises are still relevant today.

Jordan, Robert T. *Tomorrow's Library: Direct Access and Delivery.* New York: R.R. Bowker, 1970.

This discussion of the background and experiments in home delivery and mail delivery parallels the philosophy of retail stores (in the 1960s).

Kearney, Anne. "Effects of the 1976 Copyright Law." *College and Research Libraries News* 49, 5 (1988): 278–281.

Discusses the impact of the law on reserve room use and teaching methodology at University of Notre Dame; many of the faculty there thought the new reserve policy had a negative effect on the instructional process. The author feels that this experience is not unique, and additional research must be done.

Kohl, David F. *Circulation, Interlibrary Loan, Patron Use, and Collection Maintenance: A Handbook for Library Management.* Santa Barbara, Calif.: ABC-Clio, 1986.

Survey of journal literature from 1960 through 1983, with annotated bibliography.

Miller, Marilyn. "Access to Library Systems." In Sutherland, Zena, editor. *Children in Libraries: Patterns of Access to Materials and Services in School and Public Libraries.* Chicago: University of Chicago, 1981 (pp. 38–53).
Advocates establishing the appropriate resource-sharing arrangements, granting children the right to participate in them, and including children's materials and resources in the developing data system.

Morris, Leslie R. and Brautigam, Patsy. *Interlibrary Loan Policies Directory,* 3d ed. New York: Neal-Schuman, 1988.
A practical directory to be kept in internal library offices.

Morris, Leslie R.; Castle, Rosemary; and Brautigam, Patsy F. "Interlibrary Loan Policies Directory: Data from 832 Libraries." *RQ* 25, 2 (1985): 229–233.
A composite picture of loan policies for books, periodicals, and other materials, as well as information on photocopying costs and turnaround time for loan initiation. The libraries surveyed included public, academic, and special libraries. Almost all of the libraries indicated that they loaned books, but the length of the loan period varied; turnaround time was also explored.

Naismith, Rachael. "Library Service to Migrant Farm Workers." *Library Journal* 115, 4 (1989): 52–55.
This discussion of bookmobile use as an effective way of providing library services to migrant farm workers stresses the need for a commitment from the library.

Stanek, Debra J. "Videotapes, Computer Programs, and the Library." *Information Technology and Libraries* (March 1986): 42–54.
The author reviews the Copyright Act in relation to videotapes and computer software and concludes there is sufficient leeway to permit a variety of classroom and library uses. One must appreciate the rights granted to authors and understand some of the exceptions to those rights.

Tevis, Jean Ann, and Crawley, Brenda. "Reaching Out to Older Adults." *Library Journal* 113, 8 (1988): 37–40.
This discussion of the need for libraries to reevaluate their services to older adults focuses on the Topeka Public Library's commitment to such services.

Vavrek, Bernard. "Rural Road Warriors." *Library Journal* 115, 4 (1990): 56–57.

Bookmobiles provide a unique service, especially to rural patrons; this discussion provides facts and figures and concludes that there is a need for more study.

Wallace, Danny P., and Giglierano, Joan. "Microcomputers in Library." *Library Trends* 37, 3 (1989): 282–301.
Microcomputers are not just a tool for complicated, large-scale, long-term projects; they can be used to solve common everyday problems. Librarians need to be educated about them and library schools need to place greater emphasis on the development of courses on all the available technology.

Walton, Robert. "Are PC Fax Boards Good for Libraries?" *Library Journal* 115, 5 (1990): 66–68.
Questions and answers on the subject of PC Fax boards.

White, Howard S., editor. "Test Reports on 19 Facsimile Machines." *Library Technology Reports* 24, 5 (1988).
Laboratory test reports on 19 low and mid volume high speed facsimile machines.

Chapter 3

Brand, Marvine. *Security for Libraries.* Chicago: American Library Association, 1984.
An excellent source with very good articles for all kinds of libraries and a bibliography on archives and special collections, computers, detection systems, disaster, fire, insurance, law, security, theft and mutilation.

Callagham, Linda Ward. "Children's Services—What Do They Mean to the Rest of the Profession?" *American Libraries* 19, 2 (1988): 102–103.
Reviews challenges facing librarians today: Latchkey children have become common afterschool patrons of public libraries, and low literacy impacts all.

Lee, Janis M. "Confidentiality: From the Stacks to the Witness Stand." *American Libraries* 19, 6 (1988): 444–453.
A very moving personal experience of the confidentiality issue. A person on a shooting rampage killed three people; that same afternoon, only one and one half hours earlier, the person was at the public library. The director personally faced the dilemma.

Lincoln, Alan Jay. *Crime in the Library: A Study of Patterns, Impact, and Security.* New York: R.R. Bowker, 1984.

Lincoln, a professor of criminal justice, deals with the ways in which crime affects libraries but also ways library staff can have an effect on reducing crime, theft, vandalism, personal assaults, and problem patrons, and presents some practical advice based on a three-year study.

Moffett, William A., Chair. "Guidelines Regarding Thefts in Libraries [from the] RBMS Security Committee." *College and Research Library News* 49, 3 (1988): 159–162.
> Guidelines developed by the ACRL Rare Books and Manuscripts Section's Security Committee.

Morris, John. *The Library Disaster Preparedness Handbook.* Chicago: American Library Association 1986.
> Excellent discussion of basic building security, problem patrons, theft and mutilation, fire protection, water damage, preservation and conservation and insurance. Simple and inexpensive strategies are presented along with more costly and sophisticated systems.

Naylor, Alice Phoebe. "Reaching All Children: A Public Library Dilemma." *Library Trends* 35, 3 (1987): 369–392.
> Data from professional literature and from interviews with key persons in the profession describe populations of concern to children's services over the past twenty-five years. The author concludes that children's librarians and children remain second class participants within the institution and the profession, and explores how time and resource priorities are determined between services to children in the library and to adults serving children outside the library. This may be the greatest challenge facing children's specialists at the end of the twentieth century.

Romeo, Louis. "Electronic Theft Detection Systems, Part I." *Library and Archival Security* 2, 3/4 (1978). "Part II: University Libraries." 3 (Spring 1980): 1–23. "Part III: High School Libraries." 3 (Summer 1980): 1–16. "Part IV: Public Libraries." 3 (Fall-Winter 1980): 1–22. "Part V: Medical and Law Libraries." 3 (Fall-Winter 1980): 99–114.
> A survey conducted in 1976 discusses eight manufacturers of systems (by the time of publication some manufacturers were no longer marketing their products: it is interesting to see how things change).

Sable, Martin H. *The Protection of the Library and Archive: An International Bibliography.* New York: Haworth Press, 1984. (Also published in Library & Archival Security, 5, 2/3 [1983].)
> Earthquakes, electronic detection and security systems, fire, flood, insurance, mutilation, theft, vandalism, warfare, and wind damage—1085 citations.

Salter, Charles A., and Salter, Jeffrey L. *On the Frontlines: Coping with the Library's Problem Patrons.* Englewood, Colo.: Libraries Unlimited, 1988.
Deals with the problem of the mentally or emotionally disturbed patron from a psychiatric point of view, with some emphasis on the law. Clinical definitions are provided and discussions are in readable language. Includes examples of serious problems, cases with questions, outcomes, tips and related readings.

Schmidt, C. James. "Confidentiality of Library Records: Renewed Concerns." *Library Administration and Management* 2, 4 (1988): 179–180.
The author offers advice on the legal aspects: First, get the advice of informed counsel; second, your library must prepare, approve, and review local policy; third, your library must develop a set of procedures, which should contain explicit provisions for evaluating and challenging any court order.

Shuman, Bruce A. "Problem Patrons in Libraries—A Review Article." *Library & Archival Security* 9, 2 (1989): 3–19.
Reviews the recent literature and sets out the types of problem patrons, and the means of handling problems.

Simmons, Randall C. "The Homeless in the Public Library: Implications for Access to Libraries." *RQ* 25, 1 (1985): 110–120.
The homeless generally do not pose a threat to themselves or others, but may be regarded as offensive by the staff or other patrons. Six major themes are covered here: offense to others, offense to library staff, we are our own worst enemy, proper use of the library, balancing everyone's rights, and elitism—all with implications for access. The author stresses the need to understand the homeless.

Woodrum, Pat. "A Haven for the Homeless." *Library Journal* 113, 1 (1988): 55–57.
Describes the interest of one city, Tulsa, in the homeless, and how the library gave the homeless self-respect. The author writes very positively (on a generally negative subject) about the situation and the possibilities for converting homeless into a valuable resource.

Wright, Kieth C., and Davie, Judith F. *Library and Information Services for Handicapped Individuals,* 3d ed. Englewood, Colo.: Libraries Unlimited, 1989.
Details the changing scene of library service to handicapped individuals with chapters (and many references) on individuals handicapped by contagious diseases, AIDS victims, and the impact of technology on future services. The work includes specific staff development activities designed to modify attitudes and evaluate services, and specific library program and service descriptions.

Zimmerman, Lee. "Pilfering and Mutilating Library Books." *Library Journal* 86 (Oct 15, 1961): 3437–3440.
    Discusses the theft and mutilation of general and reference books and offers examples and suggestions on prevention (nonelectric), stressing a need for checkers at exits. The author concludes, however, that if someone wants to steal, they will.

Chapter 4

Bateman, Robert. "Integrated Multi-Media Libraries: At What Stage the Integration?" *The Audiovisual Librarian* 6, 2 (1980): 16–20.
    The concept of integrated shelving and storage is opposed, with reasoning.

Bookstein, Abraham. "Models for Shelfreading." *Library Quarterly* 43 (1973): 126–137.
    This difficult to read article presents a mathematical model applied to determining shelf-reading frequency and how much time should be set aside for the job. The author determines that one should be able to shelf-read 600 volumes per hour; managers must balance the cost of shelf-reading with the cost of misshelved books.

Buckland, Michael. *Book Availability and the Library User.* New York: Pergamon Press, 1975.
    A theoretical analysis that is difficult to read.

Desroches, Richard A., and Rudd, Marie. "Shelf Space Management: A Microcomputer Application." *Information Technology and Libraries* 2, 2 (1983): 187–189.
    An example of one of the first microcomputer applications of spreadsheet software.

Ellis, Judith Compton. "Planning and Executing a Major Bookshift/Move Using an Electronic Spreadsheet." *College & Research Library News* 49, 5 (1988): 282–287.
    The electronic worksheet as major planning tool for a major move; includes formulas, lots of numbers, examples, and diagrams.

Ensor, Pat; Tribble, Judy; Norman, O. Gene; and Baker, Sally. "Strategic Planning in an Academic Library." *Library Administration & Management* 2, 3 (1988): 145–149.
    Describes how an Indiana State University Library Strategic Planning Task Force developed a five-year plan, recognizing that the document is not the end. The authors acknowledge it's an ongoing process.

Greenfield, Jane. *Books: Their Care and Repair.* New York: H.W. Wilson, 1983.
> An excellent, very informative, basic manual for all who face the problem of how to repair and care for print materials. A hands-on book, with diagrams and glossary.

Henderson, Kathryn Luther, and Henderson, William T., editors, *Conserving and Preserving Library Materials.* Allerton Park Institute, 27. Urbana: University of Illinois Graduate School of Library Science, 1983.
> Papers delivered at an institute on archival preservation of nonpaper and paper-based materials, and conservation efforts.

Hubbard, William J. *Stack Management.* Chicago: American Library Association, 1981.
> A revision of William Jesse's 1952 publication, *Shelf Work in Libraries,* which dealt with the problems of collection management in the postwar era. The scope is not limited to libraries of one size or type in this excellent practical guide, which covers nonprint materials as well.

Kaempf, Kathi, and Eandi, Eileen. "Training and Supervision of Library Shelvers." *Bulletin of the Medical Library Association* 63, 3 (1975): 319–323.
> The University of Southern California Norris Medical Library uses audiovisual methods to train shelvers, and also uses detailed assignment sheets with realistic assignments. Slide/script training is encouraged.

Kountz, John. "Industrial Storage Technology Applied to Library Requirements." *Library Hi Tech* 5, 4 (1987): 13–22.
> Applied techniques and systems have been developed for warehouse operations in libraries (storing a growing mass of little used but valuable materials). The author presents an automated storage and retrieval system.

Kurth, William H., and Grim, Ray W. *Moving a Library.* New York: Scarecrow Press, 1966.
> The factors with which most libraries have to cope when moving a library, along with considerable statistical data. Both authors have a lot of experience with moving.

Mann, Thomas J. "A System for Processing and Shelving Works of Mixed Media Format." *Library Resources & Technical Services* 23, 2 (1979): 163–167.
> Gives the guidelines used at Louisiana State University Library for processing and shelving integrated and segregated collections, the principle being, "if there is no space problem, integrate."

Maxin, Jacquelin A. "The Open Shelving of Journals on Microfilm." *Special Libraries* 66, 12 (1975): 592–594.
  After favorable results with a limited test run of putting microfilm with the bound journals, the entire microfilm collection was put in open shelving. Feedback showed that microfilm open shelving had an advantage over cabinet storage and is less complicated than expected. For small academic and research libraries.

Meinke, Darrell M. "Pulling the Rug Out from Under the Stacks (Revisited)." *College and Research Libraries News* 49, 5 (1988): 288–289.
  The Moorhead State University director of facilities management designed and built a stack moving system for the library: it actually moved the stacks, materials and all.

Metz, Paul, and Litchfield, Charles A. "Measuring Collections Use at Virginia Tech." *College and Research Libraries* 49, 6 (1988): 501–513.
  Data on circulation and in-house use, figuring in kinds of use, variations in measurement technique, and time period. Three day samples of circulation volume showed statistics were stable. Some of the findings may be applicable to other libraries.

Moreland, Rachel S. "Managing Library Stacks Space with a Microcomputer." *Small Computers in Libraries* 7, 6 (1987): 38–41.
  Gives an example of using electronic spreadsheets, stressing the need for accurate information at the beginning, and describes the use of SuperCalc3 to create two spreadsheets.

Morse, Phillip, and Chen, Ching-chih. "Using Circulation Desk Data to Obtain Unbiased Estimates of Book Use." *Library Quarterly* 45, 2 (1975): 179–194.
  A difficult to read article with many formulas and statistical models for any collection in any library.

Peacock, P.G. "Measuring a Library." *Aslib Proceedings* 35, 3 (1983) 152–155.
  Presents a method for estimating occupied shelf space, using amounts 1.0, .75, .5, .25. Inspect each shelf! The superiority of measuring over estimating is stressed.

Pederson, Wayne A. "Statistical Measures for Shelf Reading in an Academic Health Sciences Center Library." *Bulletin of the Medical Library Association* 77, 2 (1989): 219–222.
  A detailed time study on shelf-reading of an entire library concludes that 902 volumes per hour is possible. James H. Sweetland responded to the article: "Letters to the Editor," *Bulletin of the Medical Library Association* 78, 1 (1990), raising questions as to why his study showed a

shelf-reading rate of 600 volumes per hour vs. 900 volumes in Pederson article.

Perk, Lawrence J., and Pullis, Noelle Van. "Periodical Usage in an Education-Psychology Library." *College and Research Libraries* 38, 3 (1977): 304–308.
The library's closed reserve system provided data (in the previous 10 years of 804 journal titles) that were analyzed according to use: Loan period, binding, multiple copies, closed reserve, and indexing services were considered. Concluded that high use titles should have shorter loan periods.

Pontius, Jack E. "The Current Periodicals Room Reconsidered." *Serials Review.* (Spring 1989): 49–54.
Describes the decision making process and subsequent efforts at Pennsylvania State University Libraries to redesign the current periodicals area to better meet patrons' needs; 12 years of 5,458 journals are now in the room.

Prostano, Emanuel T., and Prostano, Joyce S. *The School Library Media Center,* 4th ed. Littleton, Colo.: Libraries Unlimited, 1987.
This textbook for school library media center librarians discusses shelving, storage, equipment, budget, and facilities; there is not much mention of circulation control.

Reynolds, Anne L.; Schrock, Nancy C.; and Walsh, Joanna. "Preservation: The Public Library Response." *Library Journal* 114, 3 (1989): 128–132.
The authors describe a survey, and database analysis techniques performed in a public library, dealing with preservation issues, and suggest applying the survey to other public libraries. They advocate that preservation and collection maintenance funding be part of a library's responsibility. Public libraries cannot escape the preservation problems that affect all collections.

Seiler, Susan L., and Robar, Terri J. "Reference Service vs. Work Crews: Meeting the Needs of Both During a Collection Shift." *Reference Librarian* 19 (1987): 327–339.
This step-by-step, very detailed description of how over 7000 reference collection volumes were shifted in four days demonstrates the importance of preparedness. The authors claim there was no disruption of services.

Steiner, George A. *Strategic Planning.* New York: Free Press, 1979.
Excellent book on strategic planning.

Sutherland, C. Tom. "Robots in the Library." *Library Hi Tech* 5, 4 (1987): 101–102.
    With current technologies, a robot could be built that is capable of reshelving books, but not in an open stack library.

Swartzburg, Susan G. *Preserving Library Materials: A Manual.* Metuchen, N.J.: Scarecrow, 1980.
    A clearly written, pragmatic overview of the care, handling, and storage of sound recordings, videotapes, art originals, maps, photographs, slides, and microforms.

Thune, Stanley S., and House, Robert J. "Where Long-Range Planning Pays Off." *Business Horizons* 13, 4 (1970): 81–87.
    Examines the effect of planning on economic performance for businesses.

Watkins, Steven G. "Space Planning and Collection Analysis with Enable." *Library Software Review* 6, 6 (1987): 367–368.
    Spreadsheet software for library space planning: Discusses the use of Enable, an integrated software program, to develop a set of interrelated spreadsheets that model a collection and can be used for the allocation of shelf space allowing for variable rates of growth in different subject areas.

Weihs, Jean. *Accessible Storage of Nonbook Materials.* Phoenix: Oryx, 1984.
    An advocate of the integration and intershelving of print and nonprint materials, the author gives the philosophy behind it, includes practical advice on packaging, shelving, care and handling of each type, and describes the integration.

Chapter 5

Cohen, Lucy R. "Conducting Performance Evaluations." *Library Trends* 38, 1 (1989): 40–52.
    Reviews the reasons for conducting performance evaluations and the concerns and potential pitfalls in them and provides an in-depth description of a goals-based performance evaluation system. The main objective is to establish communication between the supervisor and employee in areas of responsibility, desired results and outcomes, priorities, development, and evaluation of work performed.

Duda, Frederick. "Labor Relations." In Creth, Sheila, and Duda, Frederick, editors. *Personnel Administration in Libraries.* New York: Neal-Schuman, 1981; pp. 119–188.

An excellent article, discussing unions, collective bargaining, grievance, and discipline. It is a little out of date, what with changes in the law, but it provides valuable background.

Fuller, F. Jay. "Evaluating Student Assistants as Library Employees." *College & Research Library News* 51, 1 (1990): 11–13.
How one library appraises student workers with formal confidential evaluations at least twice a year, keeping in mind that student workers' first priority is school.

Hafner, Arthur W., and Kibble-Smith, Brian G. "Managerial Responsibility for Employee Discipline." *Library Journal* 113, 8 (1988): 41–44.
Business management techniques of corrective action and employee discipline can be applied to library operations. The author discusses the right to discipline, the importance of orientation and training, performance measurement, corrective strategies, termination, and fairness. Very informative.

Holman, Norman. "Collective Bargaining in Public Libraries: Preserving Management Prerogatives." *Library Trends* 38, 1 (1989): 11–20.
Chronology of collective bargaining in Ohio, using Ohio law as a source for discussing basic information about labor relations procedures, including dispute resolution, alternative dispute resolution, interest arbitration, and management rights.

Jay, Antony. "How to Run a Meeting." *Harvard Business Review* 54, 2 (1976): 43–57.
Very informative and practical article on types of meetings, why have them, etc.

Miller, Laurence. "The Role of Circulation Services in the Major University Library." *College and Research Libraries* 34 (Nov. 1973): 463–471.
After surveying 103 academic libraries, the author concludes that circulation work does not need professionals. Circulation is a unit concerned solely with technical functions of physical dissemination and control of collections.

Neal, James G. "Employee Turnover and the Exit Interview." *Library Trends* 38, 1 (1989): 32–39.
The exit interview is an effective tool for determining the causes of turnover in a library. It should be based on standardized format, assure confidentiality, be conducted by an effective interviewing staff, and provide feedback to management.

Osterman, Paul. "Rethinking the American Training System." *Social Policy* (Summer 1988): 28–35.

Stressing the need to develop a new and stronger rationale for public investment in employment and training, one which broadens the constituency for these programs, the author says we must reorganize the system.

Riggs, Donald E. *Strategic Planning for Library Managers.* Phoenix: Oryx Press, 1984.
> This introduction to library planning presents general and basic information.

Thompson, Ronelle K.H. "Volunteers in Academic Libraries." *Library Personnel News* 2, 3 (1988): 36.
> A brief discussion on volunteers in the academic library (brief because academic libraries do not usually use volunteers).

Warner, Alice Sizer. "Using Volunteers in Libraries." *Library Personnel News* 2, 3 (1988): 33–34.
> Pros and cons of the use of volunteers.

Wells, Linda Bennett. "Volunteers in the School Media Center." *Library Personnel News* 2, 3 (1988): 34–36.

Young, Betty. "Circulation Service—Is It Meeting the User's Needs?" *Journal of Academic Librarianship* 2, 3 (1976): 120–125.
> Stress the importance of a professional librarian at the circulation desk, one who can detect the problems and the needs of users. This would improve image of the librarian and increase the satisfaction of the patron.

Chapter 6

See Brand, Marvine, *Chapter 3*

Dahlgren, Anders C., issue editor. "Library Buildings." *Library Trends* 36, 2 (1987).
> Contents include: Raymond M. Holt—Trends in Public Library Buildings; Nancy R. McAdams—Trends in Academic Library Facilities; Elaine Cohen and Aaron Cohen—Trends in Special Library Buildings; Jim Bennett—Trends in School Library Media Facilities, Furnishings, and Collections; Bradley A. Waters and Willis C. Winters—On the Verge of a Resolution: Current Trends in Library Lighting; Fred Dubin—Mechanical Systems and Libraries; Lamar Veatch—Toward the Environmental Design of Library Buildings; John Vasi—Trends in Staff Furnishings for Libraries; B. Franklin Hemphill—Alternatives to the Construction of a New Library; Nolan

Lushington—Output Measures and Library Space Planning; Marlys Cresap Davis—Reutilizing Existing Library Space; Richard B. Hall—Trends in Financing Public Library Buildings; Richard L. Waters—The Library Building of Tomorrow; and Walter C. Allen—Selected References.

See Morris, John, *Chapter 3*

Weaver-Meyers, Pat L., and Ramsey, Stephen D. "Fines for Food: A Citation System to Control Food and Drink Consumption in the Library." *College & Research Library News* 51, 6 (1990): 536–538.
  Discusses fining patrons who bring food or drink into the library at the University of Oklahoma.

Chapter 7

Camp, John A.; Agnew, Grace; Landram, Christina; Richards, Jane; and Shelton, Judith M. "Survey of Online Systems in U.S. Academic Libraries." *College and Research Libraries* 48, 4 (1987): 339–350.
  The survey produced responses from 210 libraries of various sizes; 15 percent had no online systems, 16.2 percent had no additional ones for future; cataloging and interlibrary loan are most frequently automated.

Kohl, David. "Circulation Professionals: Management Information Needs and Attitudes." *RQ* 23, 1 (1983): 81–86.
  Details a survey of circulation professionals to determine their use of attitudes toward, and sources of information about, management data and the formal techniques by which data are generated. The author found that circulation professionals perceive a greater need for such data and techniques than their institutions do; data provided by others are considered more important than information on the techniques for generating one's own data.

Nelson, Mary Ann. "Emerging Legal Issues for Library Administrators Preparing for the 1990s—A Bibliographic Essay." *Library Administration & Management* 2, 4 (1988): 188–190.
  Highlights current legal issues in employment practices. Includes discussion of the Civil Rights Act (sex discrimination), the Rehabilitation Act of 1973 (AIDS), Defamation and Invasion of Privacy (negative references, lie detectors, drug testing), Age Discrimination, and Occupational Safety and Health.

Roosevelt, Thomas R., Jr. "From Affirmative Action to Affirming Diversity." *Harvard Business Review* 2 (March–April 1990): number 90213.

An excellent article on managing diversity, set in the business world but very applicable to libraries. It concludes with an exploration to "develop capacity to accept, incorporate and empower the diverse human talents of the most diverse nation on earth."

Periodicals

American Libraries. Chicago: American Library Association, 1970– . 11/year.

Bulletin of the Medical Library Association. Baltimore: The Association, 1911– . Quarterly.

Byte. Petersborough, N.H.: Byte Pub., 1975– . Monthly.

College and Research Libraries. Chicago: American Library Association, 1939– . Bimonthly.

College and Research Library News. Chicago: American Library Association, 1966– . 11/year.

Information Technology and Libraries. Chicago: Library and Information Technology Association (of the American Library Association), 1982– . Quarterly.

Journal of Academic Librarianship. Ann Arbor: Mountainside, 1975– . Bimonthly.

Journal of Interlibrary Loan & Information Supply. New York: Haworth Press, 1990– . Quarterly

Journal of Library Administration. New York: Haworth Press, 1980– . Quarterly.

Library Administration and Management. Chicago: Library Administration and Management Association (of the American Library Association), 1987– . Quarterly.

Library & Archival Security. New York: Haworth Press, 1978– . Quarterly.

Library High Tech. Ann Arbor: Pierian Press, 1983– . Quarterly.

Library Journal. New York: Bowker, 1876– . Semimonthly, except monthly in July and August.

Library Resources & Technical Services. Chicago: American Library Association, 1957– . Quarterly.

Library Software Review. Westport, Conn.: Meckler, 1982– . Quarterly.

Library Systems Newsletter. Chicago: American Library Association, 1981– . Monthly.

Library Technology Reports. Chicago: American Library Association, 1965– . 6/year.

Library Trends. Urbana: University of Illinois Library School, 1952– . Quarterly.

MacUser. New York: MacUser Pub., 1985– . Monthly.

MacWorld. San Francisco: PC World Communications, 1984– . Monthly.

Online. Weston, Conn.: Online Inc., 1976– . Bimonthly.

Personal Computing. Hasbrouck Heights, N.J.: Hayden, 1976– . Monthly.

RQ. Chicago: Reference and Adult Services Division, (of the American Library Association), 1960– . Quarterly.

School Library Journal. New York: Bowker, 1954– . 10/year.

Serials Review. Ann Arbor: Pierian Press, 1975– . Quarterly.

Special Libraries. New York: Special Libraries Association, 1910– . Monthly.

Wilson Library Bulletin. New York: H.W. Wilson, 1914– . 10/year.

A USEFUL ALMANAC

The Library and Book Trade Almanac. The Bowker Annual. Compiled and edited by Filomena Simora. The 35th edition (published in 1990) covers 1990–91. New York: R.R. Bowker.

Covers many topics—copyright issues, technology, funding and grants, and special reports. Many articles and reports from the divisions of the American Library Association. Very informative.

Index